Second Edition

D1508809

The CHINESE PUZZLE

Putting

the pieces

together for a

deeper understanding

of China and

her Church

MIKE FALKENSTINE

The Chinese Puzzle
Putting the pieces together for a deeper understanding of
China and her Church

Second Edition

Published by China Resource Center Press

Unless otherwise indicated, Bible quotations are taken from the
English Standard Version of the Bible. Copyright © 2001 by
Crossway Bibles, a division of Good News Publishers.

ISBN: 978-1-936417-72-8

Printed in the United States

To contact the author:

www.chinaresourcecenter.org

华援

English translation:
"Serve China"

Acknowledgments

To God: Thanks for using me in China in ways I could have never imagined to accomplish Your will.

To my wife, Sherie: Love you! You are a great friend and I love growing old with you. My life is blessed because of you!

To my kids, Sarah Elizabeth, Isaac and Anna: It's an awesome privilege to be your Dad and to witness all that God is doing in your lives.

To W. Brad Miller, my first real mentor and a spiritual father during the formative years of my walk with Christ: Why in the world you chose an undisciplined, new Christian with zero prospects for a good job to disciple is beyond me, but I wouldn't be writing this book or have seen hundreds of thousands of Chinese come to know Christ without the impact you've had on my life.

To Dr. Danny Yu and Finn Torjesen: I thank you for your patience as I asked questions, and for giving me some of your time as you've passed along some of what you've learned through your many years of experience.

To the China Resource Center Donors: None of this would be possible without you. Thank you for your partnership!

To our Board of Directors: To stand side-by-side with me as we impact China for Christ means more to me than you'll ever know. It's my privilege to work together with you all!

Finally, to all my Chinese friends and colleagues: Thanks for allowing this curious American to sit and learn about your fabulous culture, history and nation.

Table of Contents

Introduction

"There are many wonderful Christians in the West who love China, who are praying for China, and who want to do anything to see God's cause advance in China. Many of them have ancestors and relatives who have served faithfully with great distinction as missionaries in China. Unfortunately, however, there is also much confusion and a great lack of understanding on what is happening among God's people in China. Especially among evangelical Christians in the United States, there is a love-and-hate relationship with China.... The situation is complex, and simplistic generalizations do not serve the cause of Christ well."

—*Dr. Samuel Ling, historian, theologian, and missiologist*

Writing the second edition of a book I've already written is a very interesting process. I want to keep most of the first edition, since it still has a lot of relevance in today's world. But things have changed a bit in China and I wanted to reflex that change, at least as much as I could given the format of this book. So, for those of you familiar with the first edition, there will be much of the second edition that will seem very familiar. You will see updated statistics, some updated quotes to begin chapters and if I was telling a story from the first edition and something new has happened in the story, I'll reflect that with new content.

I'm most excited, of course, about the two new chapters in this second edition. I've joked with friends in talking about the new chapters that I learned as much in researching the content as I hope to teach you about the subjects. Specifically, the new chapter on the Ethnic Minorities in China was a great learning experience for me. The reason there wasn't much content about China's Ethnic Minorities is that I didn't know that much about them when I wrote the first edition. What a fascinating aspect to China that we all need to know more about and pay attention to going forward. I hope you all agree with me that this new chapter adds a lot to the book.

As a side note, the idea to write a chapter on China's Ethnic Minorities came directly from some of you as you used the first edition to introduce people to China. So my invitation still stands: If after reading this book, you feel it's still missing something that you'd really like to see in the third edition, please let me know and I'll definitely take it under consideration.

I have felt a direct leading to help you understand China and her Church. There is much confusion. Does persecution exist? Can Christians in China worship freely? As a Westerner, how may I most effectively pray for and engage in China? Many people are confused by these questions and issues. China is like a huge puzzle, with many pieces and moving parts; it's hard to identify all that is happening today in China.

In your mind, imagine that China is a huge jigsaw puzzle. If you've ever put one together, you may have started by organizing all the pieces, perhaps by color or by size. Then, as you began to put the pieces together, you may have searched for pieces that looked similar to one another. Of course, you could always refer to the picture on the box as your guide. Imagine how much harder it would be if you didn't have the picture on the box to help you put the pieces together. How would you complete the puzzle? Could you? You may be able to put a few pieces together initially, but it would be much harder to finish the puzzle without the box as your guide. Interestingly, this analogy carries many parallels, as I observe the Western Church's perspective on Christianity in China. People are trying to describe the whole picture, when all they really have are two or three pieces of a 500-piece puzzle.

I hope you will embrace this book as your complete picture to put together the Chinese Puzzle. China is experiencing some monumental, head-spinning changes, and even the most discerning China analyst may find it daunting to keep up. Information flows from multiple sources, and much of it seems contradictory; this doesn't facilitate our understanding of China and her church. There are also some in the West who pose as 'China Experts,' even though they haven't been to China in many years, they don't speak the Chinese language, and they are therefore functioning with old paradigms which foster old stereotypes of China.

In writing this book, I hope to give you many more pieces to the puzzle that may deepen your understanding of China and thereby Christianity in China. With many more pieces to the puzzle, I believe you will be able to pray more effectively for China, engage with what God is doing there, and see China from a much more balanced perspective. As we finish the first decade of the 21st century, the situation in China is ripe for increased Western engagement based on mutual understanding, and I hope this book serves as a catalyst to strengthen and deepen that understanding.

Throughout the following nine chapters, I will attempt to clarify perceptions of China and her church. I've tried to keep this book short, even with two new chapters in this second edition, so one could read it in its entirety on a flight from North America to China, but I have also striven to thoroughly cover the main points. By the time you get off the plane, you will have finished the book, and you will be ready to engage with the Chinese culture.

Chapter one presents a history of Christianity in China and the missionary past. I think we can learn many valuable lessons as we look at the missionary effort in 19th century China. In 1905, novelist George Santayana wrote, "Those who cannot remember the past are doomed to repeat it."[1] The history of Chinese ministry has great relevance as we engage in China today. This chapter is virtually unchanged from the first edition, since events in the 19th century aren't going to change much!

Chapter two looks at the current trends that are changing China, from the inside out. These changes and developments are important for our understanding of China. This may be a surprising chapter, as you learn some of the groundbreaking efforts taking place, including the rapidly emerging Christian book publishing efforts that I detail for the first time in the second edition.

As you may know, the Chinese people have different social and moral standards than we have in the West. In Chapter three, we will examine these differences. If we want to understand China, we need to recognize their relational differences and social standards. Chapter three also investigates the Chinese view on legality and the Rule of Law.

Chapter four examines what I call the 'Persecution Myth': the false belief that Christians in China continue to suffer massive persecution for their faith in Christ. Persecution does not happen as much as we may think, and we must change our paradigm. Westerners who live in China and work with the Chinese church know that persecution is no longer the headlining story. We will look at the reasons the myth continues to persist and the organizations who don't want the myth to die.

Chapter five was born out of the intense coverage some Western ministries and Christian media have been giving to one of Beijing's over 3000 unregistered 'house' churches. In travelling regularly to Beijing, I was hearing that most of Beijing's Unregistered Churches were operating without interference with the Beijing government officials. This coverage from the West was constant, so I decided that I'd do some research. What I found will quite possibly change your opinion of not only Beijing's Unregistered Churches, but also Unregistered Churches nationwide.

For anyone who wants to become actively involved in God's work in China, Chapter six can become your guidebook for involvement. You can read about new opportunities to work transparently, a new 'industry standard' of engagement, and a practical guide for getting started in China.

Before engaging in the research of China's Ethnic Minorities to write Chapter seven, I really didn't know that much about the Minority groups in China. What I found out what not only fascinating, but also has broadened my understanding of the overall work that God is doing in China and the obstacles that lie before us as we desire to impact China for Christ. I really enjoyed learning about these groups and I hope you agree that this chapter adds a lot to the overall value of this book.

One of the other keys to our understanding of modern-day China is being able to see China and life through the eyes of the Chinese themselves. Through my work in the China Resource Center, I talk to many Americans about China. Through these countless conversations, I can see the inaccuracies in people's thoughts and perceptions about the lives of today's Chinese. By painting with broad strokes, Chapter eight will clarify the overall picture of how the Chinese view their government, life and democracy. Some of my findings may surprise you.

As you will discover through the pages of this book, I have been working with Chinese and in China for twenty years. In Chapter nine, I'll give an overview of my work in China and an introduction to the work of the China Resource Center, including a great new project that we've engaged in since the first edition of this book. I believe we have a great mission, and I'm excited to be involved.

I must also note the contents in Appendix A; It's the complete text of the Ethical Foundations for China Service, created by a number of China ministry leaders at Fuller Seminary in June 2006. This document provides a standard of best practices in China, both for China-interested organizations and individuals. I hope that you may take the Foundations into your own organization, and use it as a discussion starter and a point of dialogue about most effective practices in China. It has proved to be an invaluable tool for many organizations and I'd recommend it to anyone or any organization just starting out in China.

It was because of the warm reception of the first edition that I've written this second edition. My hope and prayer is that this book would bless many who also have a heart for China. The workers are still few in relation to the total need and I'm praying this book is used to increase the harvest! I hope it is useful for your understanding of China and her Church. Enjoy!

[1] Santayana, George. "The Life of Reason, Vol. I." Prometheus Books; New Ed Edition. 1998.

Chinese History Tells a Story

"But are we not much superior to them? Are we not more manly, more intelligent, more skillful, more humane, more civilized, nay, are we not more estimable in every way? Yes, according to our way of thinking. No, emphatically no, according to theirs. And it would be nearly as difficult for us to alter our opinion on the subject as it is for them to alter theirs."
—*Griffith John, Welsh missionary to China, 1869*

History Dies Very Slowly

I received my first taste of the Chinese perspective on history when my wife and I lived in Birmingham, Alabama, ministering to Chinese International Students at the

University of Alabama at Birmingham. We had developed friendships with many Chinese students, most of whom were in Birmingham to study at a graduate level.

We loved getting to know these Chinese friends, and we often invited them into our home for meals. We also cultivated these friendships by helping them with their transportation needs. Most university students coming from China at that time were poor and without financial resources. Although they were in their mid to late twenties, most of them had never had the opportunity to learn how to drive, and very few of them had a need for a car. Residents in Chinese cities in the 1990's were still very dependent on a bicycle and public transportation. But in a southern city in America, they learned quickly that a car was necessary for daily life. They had no clue how to drive, how to purchase a car, or how to maintain their new investment after buying one. This became a great avenue for us to serve the new residents in our city, and word spread quickly of our services and ability to meet their needs. We hosted "car care" clinics, taught many Chinese scholars how to drive (usually in an empty parking lot!), and helped several of them purchase used cars.

A surprising trend emerged as we helped these friends purchase their cars. Even though my wife and I boasted the reliability and low cost operation of the available Japanese-made cars, like Honda and Toyota, none of our Chinese friends wanted to buy these cars that were originally made in Japan. They often opted for the American-made cars, which puzzled my wife and me; at that time, the Japanese cars were a much better option, especially in the used car market.

After many transactions of this kind, I asked one of my Chinese friends why these Chinese scholars did not choose the Japanese cars. I had gotten to know this man quite well, and I considered him to be an intellectual, mild-tempered individual. He turned bright red as he considered my question. "I wouldn't give my business to the Japanese after what they did to our country, to our people!"

I did not have the knowledge of Chinese history that I have now, so I asked him to elaborate. "First, they attacked our country, and then they killed so many! I will never own a Japanese car! We (China) have never attacked another country.... We are always the one who gets attacked!" He spoke of The Nanjing Massacre, an infamous genocidal war crime committed by the Japanese against innocent Chinese in Nanjing, in 1937 and 1938. The Nanjing Massacre is so horrible because of the savage nature of the killings and the number of Chinese killed (250,000 to 300,000). The Japanese soldiers held killing games to see who could kill the most people, and many times, after the Japanese soldiers had killed the innocent Chinese, they disemboweled them as well. There exists a Nanjing Massacre Museum in Nanjing; I've visited and seen the bones of bodies stacked on top of one another, fifteen or twenty people deep.

When I first learned of The Nanjing Massacre, I was shocked to know that the Japanese had killed so many in such horrible ways. But I was also surprised to see my Chinese friend, born in the early 1970's, reacting so strongly to an event that happened thirty-five years before he was even born. In probing further, I explained to him that the Japanese companies do not receive any profit from the purchase of a used car. They only receive profit from the purchase of a new car. Still, he wouldn't hear of it. For him and many other Chinese, to own a Japanese car is the equivalent of committing high treason against their home country.

Even today, many Chinese feel that the Japanese have not shown true remorse for these wartime crimes, and feelings of anger affect many aspects of Chinese society, including Sino-Japanese relations in politics, business and trade. This illustration reflects the Chinese perspective on history. When a Chinese friend of mine traced his family lineage over 1500 years, and all of them had lived in the same village for centuries upon centuries, I acquired a new respect for the Chinese perspective of history. Many of the events portrayed in this chapter have taken place in the 19th century, a time when America was merely getting its feet wet as a new nation. Chinese history is deeper and longer, so historical events linger more with the Chinese than for some of us in the West.

History Tells a Story

One way to think of Chinese history is to compare the last 5,000 years to a 5,000-meter race. For the first 4,700 years, China was widely accepted as a world leader. Only within the last 300 years, they fell behind. Throughout Chinese history, the "Chinese thought that China alone represented true civilization; only its ruler, the Son of Heaven, deserved to sit at the apex of the hierarchy of earthly monarchs."[1] In their minds, no one eclipsed the Chinese Emperor, and there was no civilization better than the 'Middle Kingdom.' For their time, they were one of the most advanced civilizations on earth, if not the leader.

With this in mind, it is understandable that the Chinese handled their first contact with Westerners, and thereby Christianity, with deference. Before the first contact with Christian missionaries, China had a long, rich religious history. Confucianism and Daoism were well-established religions, long before the first Christian missionaries arrived in China. Confucian thinking has had a tremendous influence on the history of Chinese culture and civilization for over 2,000 years. With an emphasis on right living, strong family loyalty, looking to the ancients for guidance, and a Chinese version of the Golden Rule, Confucianism remained a mainstream Chinese orthodoxy throughout Chinese history.

Although Christian tradition often recognizes Thomas the Apostle as the first missionary in China during his travels to Persia and India, the first documented Christian missionaries arrived in China during the Tang Dynasty, the Golden Age of Chinese History. These Nestorian Christians took the overland trade route from Persia to the Tang Capital of Chang'an in 635 AD. After 200 successful years in ministry, Nestorian Christianity was virtually destroyed in a major persecution, initiated by a Tang Emperor in 845 AD.

From this point, we see a pattern in Chinese History of Christian Missionaries coming to China, leaving, and coming back again. Nestorian Christians returned to China as scribes and teachers in 1279 AD, only to be driven out again in 1353 AD. The first Europeans in China were the Portuguese, in 1515 AD. The Chinese saw no difference between them and the Japanese pirates, with whom they were very familiar. In 1518, as the Portuguese sent an embassy to Beijing, the Portuguese naval commander stayed behind in Canton, blockading the port and firing on Chinese warships. They were forced out of China, and they resorted to setting up illegal camps on small ocean islands off the coast. The Portuguese were able to set up the settlement of Macao, near Hong Kong, in 1538; Macao served as a trading port between Portugal, India, China and Japan. The Portuguese obtained a lease from Beijing in 1557, and Macao remained under Chinese sovereignty, even though their administration was Portuguese. The colony at Macao gave entrance for the next wave of Christian missionaries.

The Jesuits first landed in Macao on Portuguese ships in 1582, led by the prominent Matteo Ricci. Father Ricci spent eighteen years building bridges with the current emperor, and he won the respect of the Chinese officials. He opened doors for Jesuit scientists and philosophers by introducing Western science, mathematics, astronomy, and visual arts to the imperial court. But the Jesuits could not continue ministering to the Chinese by way of accommodation. Conflict arose over the issue of ancestor worship, and the Emperor expelled all missionaries in 1724.

The next Europeans were the Dutch, who had already traded with the Japanese for many years. They worked from their camp in Japan to try to establish contacts with the Chinese. They were never able to establish as extensive a trading relationship as the English did at Canton. With the Portuguese settlement at Macao, we begin to see a trend of Western Missionaries coming on the coattails of imperial powers. This trend came into full bloom with the arrival of the English.

The English were able to establish the most significant trading relationship with the Chinese imperial government. The East India Company (EIC), a conglomeration of London merchants, who had received a royal charter from Queen Elizabeth to monopolize all trade in the East Indies, found the most success. The EIC's first success was in India, where they set up a very profitable cotton industry. They soon established a multi-port trading system, where they bought Chinese silk and medicine from Canton, which were desirable in England. They paid for them with Indian imports like cotton and spices, which were desirable in China. This system hit its peak when the EIC began exporting tea from China to England. They had discovered a product that had widespread appeal with the English, so much so that by the eighteenth century, tea became the national beverage of England. The British crown seized this new obsession with tea, imposing a 100 percent excise duty on the EIC tea. This duty generated major revenue for the English government.

Through a series of events, the EIC could no longer pay for the tea they were exporting; they needed to find something desirable to the Chinese which would help pay for the voluminous amounts of tea. The Chinese wanted only one thing in that massive quantity: the addictive drug, opium. Opium was grown in India, and because China had outlawed the importation of opium, the EIC had to sell it through agency houses, which then sold the drug and used their profits to fund the tea trade back to Britain.

By 1820, China imported over 900 tons of opium from India through these agency houses. This led to a national epidemic of opium addicts, and in 1838, Lin Zexu, the Emperor-designated 'Drug Czar' effectively curbed the drug traffic and trade in China. In 1839, Lin imposed a trade embargo on the British, thereby prohibiting the further importation of opium, under the penalty of death. The English trade commissioner told all opium dealers to give their stock of opium to him, and he later turned it over to Lin.

In 1839, Lin also took the extraordinary step of directly petitioning Queen Victoria, questioning the moral reasoning of the royal government. Citing the strict prohibition of the opium trade within England, Ireland, and Scotland, Lin questioned how Britain could then profit from the drug in China. The British government offered no response to Lin's petition. They saw Lin as a threat to their lucrative trade, and they believed his actions were destruction of private property. Both the English government and her merchants wanted to continue opium trade, despite any moral apprehensions about supplying so many Chinese with this highly addictive drug.

This became the catalyst for the Opium War, lasting from 1839 to 1842, and leading to the defeat of the Chinese. British military superiority was clearly evident from the beginning, showing far greater advanced weaponry than the Qing government. After signing the Treaty of Nanjing in 1842, which effectively stopped the War, the British imposed on the Chinese the first of the 'Unequal Treaties', which marked the beginning of a century of imperialist exploitation. As a part of the Treaty, the Western missionary finally achieved his long sought goal of full toleration. He was no longer restricted to Canton, and he could now live in five cities along the East Coast of China. During the last half of the 19th century, more treaties brought access to even more of China, enabling travel to inland areas of China.

Christian Missionary Effort of the 19th Century

During this time period, the first Protestant missionary arrived in China. The arrival of Robert Morrison, of the London Missionary Society in 1807, fueled the next missionary attempt. In 1805, the London Missionary Society, barely ten years old, began planning a mission to the Chinese. Since the EIC was so hostile to missionaries, Morrison had to secure passage to China through the United States on an American ship. Despite the ship captain's pessimism, Morrison was determined to impact China. In this famous quote, the ship's captain asked him, "And so, Mr. Morrison, you really expect to make an impression on the idolatry of the great Chinese empire?"

Morrison replied, "No, sir, I expect God will."

He had started Chinese language study while he was a student in London, and he continued his language study in Canton (now Guangzhou). He was the first Protestant missionary to live in China, and he was a great student of the Chinese language. Morrison is widely known as the Father of Protestant Missions in China, and he opened the doors for many other missionaries in China, including J. Hudson Taylor. By 1809, in order to secure his position in China, Morrison took a job with the previously inhospitable EIC, as a translator.

The Protestant missionaries of the 19th century were dedicated to reaching China for Christ. Their zeal and enthusiasm for their calling was impressive. Many missionaries were willing to surrender their lives for the good of the Gospel effort in China, and a number of them did. One such American missionary was S. Rowena Bird, who was persecuted during the Boxer Rebellion and many other uprisings in the 19th century. Bird exemplifies the missionary commitment of the day. In a letter to her family during the height of the Boxer rebellion, she wrote, "If you never see me again, remember I am not sorry I came to China."[2]

Many of these missionaries faced numerous difficulties and hardships. They served in an era when standard coinage and banking facilities were nearly non-existent, which made the transmission, handling and recording of funds very difficult. A general lack of postal and telegraphic services stymied efficient administration and communications. The evangelization of the Chinese was primary on their minds, and they envisioned a thriving Christian church, much like the Churches they had left behind in Liverpool or Chicago. Among their biggest challenges was Chinese resistance to the Gospel, especially among the educated class. With few exceptions, this class steadfastly refused to even sympathize with the religion, much less embrace it.

Robert Morrison also served as an example of these missionaries' commitment and benefit as the first Westerners to learn Mandarin Chinese. His work as a translator for Western merchants gained him legitimate residence in Canton, allowing him time to pursue his most significant work. Morrison's work on the printed page was his main contribution to the long-term Christian effort in China. He laid a foundation that his later successors built upon.

He had an unusual capacity for large quantities of hard work. Even as he was translating for the EIC, he also prepared and translated Christian literature. By 1819, with the aid of the Scotsman, W. C. Milne, he completed the translation of the Old and New Testaments. Morrison also wrote and compiled a six-volume Chinese/English dictionary, which became the preeminent dictionary for English-speaking people.

Many additional missionaries came to China during this time, both English and American. America's first missionary to China, Elijah C. Bridgman, came to China in 1830. In 1854, J. Hudson Taylor arrived to work with the China Evangelization Society. After six years of working with other missionaries, working on his own Chinese language study, and later taking over a hospital in Ningbo, Taylor returned to England in 1860, due to poor health. This season turned out to be most significant in England, as the first great wave of the frontier missionary advance. In the British Isles, Taylor spent much of his time speaking about China and her needs. He also finished his medical degree, and he became friends with Charles Spurgeon, who became his lifelong friend and supporter.

Missionary Response to Opium and War

In the midst of the missionaries' obvious zeal for Christ's work in China, their attitudes simultaneously hampered their work in China, thereby tainting Christianity in the minds of many Chinese. Throughout the mid-1800's, a persistent theme emerged from American missionary literature: some believed that normal diplomacy was unworkable with the Chinese, because they only understood and responded to force during moments of crisis.

Even before the first Opium War, the *Chinese Repository* published similar advice. Edited by American missionaries Elijah C. Bridgman and Samuel W. Williams, the publication carried consistent themes that the 'imbecilic' Chinese "will insult so long as they meet no resistance, but when force is opposed to force, their courage fails." Force alone would "break down their minds" and abandon their "haughty isolation." Apparently, the concept of national sovereignty did not apply, as far as these missionaries were concerned.

In addition, many missionaries of this time period supported the use of force against China, in order to open the doors for the Gospel. "How these difficulties do rejoice my heart because I think the English government may be enraged, and God, in His power may break down the barriers which prevent the Gospel of Christ from entering China," said Henrietta Shuck, the first female American missionary to China, during the buildup before the Opium War.

Rev. W. J. Boone shared in this sentiment. As the Royal Navy finally materialized off China's Coast, Boone declared, "There is but one single barrier to the establishment of hundreds of missions among the literally perishing heathen idolaters, and that barrier is of a political nature, which might be removed in a day." Standing in contrast to the missionaries' zeal was a growing intensity of the tradition of Chinese hostility toward Christianity.

To understand this call of force, we must acquire a couple of key pieces to the puzzle. First, we see a change in power in world affairs during the 19th century, with the crumble of the Chinese empire and the ascendancy of the British as the most powerful country in the world. This was also a time of great discovery and imagination. The United States was a growing world power; American citizens believed that anything was possible. Also, we must recognize the consistent calls and justification for armed force amongst missionaries, in terms of a widely held 19th century missionary theory, called the 'domino theory.' In their thinking, China was the key to worldwide salvation, as Satan's chief fortress. The conversion of her immense population would overthrow pagan defenses elsewhere throughout the world, ushering in the millennium. Biblical warnings, including statements that the defeat of Satan's kingdom would involve turmoil and bloodshed, made it easier for the missionaries to accept martyrdom. The slaughter of countless thousands of "Satan's willing servants" by Western forces translated into actions divinely inspired and directed.

To their credit, Christian missionaries were nearly unanimous in their opposition to the opium trade, and they initially applauded Lin Zexu's actions. Williams hoped that the English would recognize the righteousness of this act, but some of his colleagues hoped that England would respond by initiating war, to open avenues for the Gospel in China. Through the pages of the *Christian Repository*, Bridgman had become one of the foremost critics of the opium trade in the

1830's; he saw the increased devastation on the Chinese population. He published over thirty articles or essays showing the evil influence of the opium trade on the political, moral and commercial health of the nation. These missionaries needed to resolve the quandary presented by the evils of the opium trade, instead of breaking down, by force of arms, the restrictions placed on evangelical efforts in China, since the English/Allied power of force fueled both efforts.

To answer such doubts, they often minimized the opium issue. They stated that God's methods were strange, but they were confident that in His own chosen way, He would end the opium trade. Although they agreed that the opium trade was inhuman, they reasoned that man cannot easily understand God's ways, and God could use whatever means He chose to open the doors of China, even His enemies. This rationalization was key for missionaries during the Opium War. Between 1840 and 1900, these missionaries unanimously viewed almost every Western invasion of China as an act of Providence. In the spirit of ecumenicalism, the Southern Baptists J. Lewis and Henrietta Shuck, Congregationalists Bridgman and Parker, and the Episcopalian Boone, all joined in agreement with Williams. They believed the war in Asia was the scheme "of the God of nations....to open a highway for those who would preach the Word."

"I am constrained," Medical missionary Peter Parker wrote, "to look back upon the present state of things not so much as an opium or an English affair, as the great design of Providence to make the wickedness of man subserve His purpose of mercy toward China in breaking through her wall of exclusion."[3]

When opium smuggling continued after the Opium War, the missionaries' consciences were further troubled. "We have taught all Asia, if not to love us, at least to dread us...to acknowledge our power....let us now show that we are a nation of Christians," said Boone.[4] American missionaries also began to receive mild criticism from home, mainly in religious journals. The *Christian Examiner* warned, "While God may turn evil to good, the character of evil and the evildoer remains unchanged." The Chinese saw the British government, who brought the opium trade and its evils to China, as the expression of Christian morality. Despite the criticisms that missionaries expressed against the British government over the opium trade, A. E. Moule, of the China Missionary Society, admitted, "The opium trade is a Christian monopoly. Its history is a Christian sin, a Christian shame: and it blocked grievously the reception of Christianity by the Chinese." [5]

The Boxer Rebellion

By the late 1890's, the anti-foreigner sentiment was growing amongst many Chinese, and aggression against foreigners occurred in China with increasing frequency. Foreign missionaries in the interior of China often bore the brunt of these attacks. China had been subject to at least six different foreign dominated treaties, each of which gave more rights to the foreigner and fewer rights to the Chinese. The Chinese regarded these treaties as very unfair, and rumors began circulating that foreigners were committing crimes as a result of the agreements within the treaties. Further, a growing number of Chinese Christians used the cloak of foreign protection to mask criminal activity. When Chinese authorities pursued these criminals, they conveniently hid behind foreign enclaves.

In addition, after many years of effort, the Roman Catholic Church got their Bishop's official ranking within the Chinese Government. In their local areas, they were not only Catholic Bishops, but they also had power within their local government. This was especially offensive to a gentry's social class, who used status in local governments. Catholic missionaries also acquired the right to freely preach and practice religion anywhere in the Chinese empire, under the effective protection of Chinese authorities. The Catholic Church also used this power to prohibit many Chinese rituals and traditions, such as ancestor worship. Desperate Chinese citizens began to band together, determined to fight what seemed to be an avalanche of problems at the hands of the foreigner. Such animosity resulted in civil disobedience and violence towards both foreigners and Chinese Christians.

One Chinese group, the Righteous Harmony Society (or the Boxers, as they later became known), became the main organized society for anyone unhappy with the current downward trends of the time. Empress Dowager, whose power had weakened, could do nothing as the Boxers first attacked the foreign enclaves in Beijing and Tianjin in June 1900. In order to protect their countrymen, foreign armies were dispatched from several nations, including Japan, Russia, Germany, England, and the United States. In all, over 55,000 troops subverted the angry Boxers. At the end of the conflict, 230 non-Chinese were killed, as well as many more Chinese converts, mainly in Shandong and Shanxi provinces.

In the wake of the Boxer Rebellion, the multi-country force that contributed to the troop deployment forced the Empress to sign the 'Boxer Protocol', also known as Peace Agreement between the Eight-Nation Alliance and China. The protocol called for China to pay 450 million taels of Silver (about $335 million gold dollars) in reparations, and they had to allow the eight nations to base their troops in Beijing. The financial reparations were a difficult burden on the common Chinese, who had to foot the bill for the reparations with increased taxes. At the time, the Qing Government's budget was only 250 million taels of silver. They added the Empress to their war criminals list, although she probably had very little to do with the Rebellion.

The aftermath of the Boxer Rebellion also left the Qing Government weaker and less able to control the country, with no answers on how to strengthen China again to defend itself against foreign subjugation. Ironically, this situation only worsened their plight.

After the alliance troops secured a decisive victory against the rebellion, the bloodthirsty tone of American missionaries' cries for vengeance reached a new level. American Missionary Henry Porter praised the German soldiers as agents of God. In the eyes of Porter, it seems clear that the proper way to deal with the Chinese was to burn, kill and loot, all in an effort to demonstrate what the missionaries wanted to communicate all along.

The Nazarene Rev. D. Z. Sheffield explained, "It is not bloodthirstiness in missionaries to desire to see further shedding of blood, and an understanding of Chinese character and conditions, and a realization that the policy of general forgiveness means the loss of many valuable native and foreign lives."[6] Some American missionaries, certain of the righteousness of their position, communicated their opinions to the American press. They readily agreed to interviews, and they sent open letters to editors of lay and religious publications, as well as to the Associated Press.

Two bishops' vindictive statements upon their return from China evoked critical editorials. "It is worth any cost in money, it is worth any cost in bloodshed if we can make millions of Chinese true and intelligent Christians."[7] The editor of the San Francisco Call correctly countered, "These two bishops make a sorry spectacle of the kind of Christianity that we seem to be exporting to Asia in carload lots."[8]

In publishing their thoughts on the Chinese Boxer situation, the missionaries had a very bad sense of timing. Just as they were communicating their sentiments, news came back from China of mass murder, rape, and looting on the part of the Allied troops. As the headlines announced that the German Kaiser commanded his troops to 'give no quarter' in China, the New York Sun quoted an American missionary: "The Germans have the right idea: punish the Chinese first and treat with them later."[9] That newspaper reporter also felt compelled to give this background explanation: "Such a remark from a missionary might seem a bit surprising to persons away from Peking, but it expresses the common sentiment here." This was the stark reality: for every missionary slain at the hands of the Boxers, a thousand Chinese men, women and children were killed by the Allied forces.

God at Work in China

The aftermath of the Boxer Rebellion also presented difficulties for the Christian effort. The Chinese believed that the indemnity obligations were unfair, and even though mission organizations kept their claims low, they were lumped in with the inequity of Western demands. In this context of Chinese hatred, the missionaries tried to live out their callings as messengers of the Gospel. After the Treaty of Nanjing, the protestant effort really began to blossom. By 1900, they had 100,000 Chinese Christians and almost 3,800 missionaries. This missionary movement was fueled primarily by Hudson Taylor's call for a new wave of missionaries to commit their lives to reaching China.

Together with his wife, he wrote *China's Spiritual Needs*, a book that would become one of God's vehicles for this great missionary advance. It was a manifesto of his life and work, and it described in great detail the desperate lack of Protestant Chinese missionaries in China. The book was reprinted several times over a thirty-year period, and it became the prime recruitment tool for the birth of a new missionary agency: China Inland Mission. Later, many gave credit to the book for fostering the widest evangelistic campaign since the time of the Apostle Paul. In the book, Taylor paints a very compelling picture of the 400 million Chinese, the vast majority of whom had never heard the name of Christ. He called for twenty-four missionaries to come to China, to reach the inland provinces; this created a new organization, the China Inland Mission (CIM).

This new wave of missionaries came to China with a faith and commitment, refusing to be intimidated by massive hindrance. By January 1911, the China Inland Mission had 968 workers (including wives) reaching into the inland provinces of China. Throughout the last half of the 19th century, these CIM missionaries, together with missionaries from other organizations, established a three-fold approach to missions work: medical, educational, and evangelistic. They established schools and hospitals, and they eventually opened thirteen Christian universities.

During this period of Chinese missionary efforts, Hudson Taylor stands out as a shining light in contrast to prevailing missionary attitudes. Known for his sensitivity to Chinese culture and his zeal for evangelism, he is one of the greatest missionaries of all time, and he is one of the most influential foreigners ever to come to China in the 19th century. Taylor was the first Western missionary to adopt Chinese dress habits. This became a staple for CIM missionaries, who stood in contrast to other British missionaries, trying to preserve British ways of life by remaining in Western clothing. This decision was Taylor's way of blending in with the Chinese, as he was convinced that the Gospel would only take root in Chinese soil if missionaries were willing to affirm the culture of the people they sought to reach.

During the Boxer Rebellion, which troubled him greatly, Taylor refused to accept payment for loss of property or life, to show the 'meekness and gentleness of Christ'. Though some criticized him, he would not have it any other way. He was also instrumental in the beginning of 'faith missions' movement, a recruitment practice that guarantees no missionary a salary, but relied on God to move in the hearts of men for provision. That practice is still in use today, among many mission organizations.

Conclusion

In the 19th century, each crisis in China provoked the missionaries' belief that the Chinese were unable to understand or respond to anything other than force. Their justification of British aggression before 1870 reflected bitter despair over the lack of success in seeing significant numbers of Chinese people come to know Christ. Believing that the real barrier was political, these missionaries were conditioned to expect dramatic results in the wake of each British and allied invasion. After each invasion, as their high expectations did not come to fruition, they hailed the next armed attack to punish those who mocked the Gospel truth. However, after 1870, the Protestant missionary movement in China found relatively greater success. Under the protection of the treaties, missionary work moved out of the Eastern port cities and into the inland provinces of China. With only 8,000 converts in 1870, that number climbed dramatically to nearly 100,000 converts by the end of the century.

The 20th century ushered in what has been called Christianity's Golden age in China. It was a time of transition and change, for both the church and the nation. China moved from dynastic rule to a republic, then to the Guomindang and Chinese Communist party. Christianity enjoyed widespread popularity for two decades. A varied Christian community grew, in which conservative, evangelical societies popped up around the country. Chinese reaction to the Boxer Rebellion led many Chinese to believe that reform was necessary, and they looked to the West to help them take the necessary steps to reform. Christianity gained new favor as missionaries taught the truth that Western progress came from its Christian heritage. Christian schools, missionaries, and their writings were open sources of information. Parochial schools filled and developed a group of Chinese Christian leaders, who gained influential positions in government and academia.

As we assess the missions effort in the 19th century in China, what lessons can we learn? There is certainly a perplexing aspect as to the nature by which history is portrayed in the 19th century in China. I hesitate to make too many bold statements, since many others know this information better than I do. But certainly, for our understanding of modern-day China, I'd like to give you a few key pieces to the puzzle.

Surprisingly, it appears that very few missionaries of the 19th century found it strange that Christ's good news arrived in China by way of armed force with guns and cannons. As I will share in later chapters, I believe strongly in taking the time to understand the Chinese and allowing them to teach me about China. These Western missionaries seemed to have an insensitivity of cultural and historical understanding. This insensitivity continually hampered their efforts to share Christ with the Chinese. In the Chinese mind, the show of force, which led to humiliation, was inexorably tied to Christianity. After all, the missionaries' home countries brought their armies to China.

As we recognize this correlation in the minds of the Chinese, we must also remember how slowly history dies in China. We can learn a great deal about this as we pursue our understanding of modern-day China. Over the last thirty years, many Westerners have come to China with an attitude of 'we know best'. This attitude never serves us well in China. In 1 Corinthians 9, the Apostle Paul commands, "For though I am free from all, I have made myself a servant to all, that I might win more of them. To the Jews, I became as a Jew, in order to win Jews." In the same way, we could also say, "To the Chinese I became as a Chinese, in order to win Chinese." Of course, those of us of Anglo ancestry will never become just like the Chinese; but at the heart of the matter, we can understand their culture, learn their language, and enter our situation in China with the heart of a learner.

It is easy to criticize the 19th century Western missionaries, but a look at history gives further perspective. When Robert Morrison arrived in China in 1807, China was an isolationist country raked with serious problems in infrastructure, government systems, and social programs. Through apparently less-than-ideal circumstances, God clearly used the Western powers and their missionaries to accomplish His plan in China. The growth of the Church in China bears testimony to His work.

One of the more interesting pieces of this growth has to do with what happened to the Chinese Church when the Communist government took power in 1949. Through the course of the first half of the 20th century, many missionaries worried about the slow development of the Chinese to take ownership of the Church. Missionary church planters hoped that a church would sustain itself to reach China for Christ. When the Communists took power, there were about 70,000 Chinese Christians. For the next thirty years, no foreigners were involved in the development of the Church in China, and many outside of China wondered what would happen to the Church. It wasn't until 1978 that anyone from outside of China could get back in to see what had happened.

Their findings were astonishing! Under severe persecution and without the help or support of the Western world, the Chinese church had grown to nearly 1 million Christian believers. Clearly, God combined the best intentions and the worst mistakes of Western missionaries, and He used it all to develop His church in China. So, could early Western missionaries have done some things differently? Definitely, yes! Did they hamper God's plan for China with their Western superiority complex? No! And did God honor their commitment to surrender their lives for God's work in China? Without question!

Missionaries of the 19th century came to China as spiritual reformers, but perhaps their bigger impact came in the social and material improvements they pioneered. As the

Communist Party took power in 1949, the missionaries stressed a number of projects: the spread of literacy to common people; the publication of journals and pamphlets in the vernacular; education and equality for women; the abolition of arranged child-marriages; increased agricultural productivity through the sinking of wells and improved tools, crops and breeds; dike and road building for protection against flood and famine; public health clinics to treat common ailments and prevent disease. Missionaries of the 19th century pioneered all of these activities, setting the groundwork for the improvement of the nation of China.

As American missionary W. J. Boone stated at the beginning of the Opium War, "We may err, but it is an error for which God will surely forgive us." Certainly, God forgave them, and He used them in mighty ways to set the foundation for the work of the Gospel in China.

[1] Wakeman, Frederick. *The Fall of Imperial China.*, Jr., p 111.
[2] Ambassadors for Christ Boxer Rebellion Martyr Poster, 2007.
[3] Miller, Stuart Creighton. "Ends and Means." *The Missionary Enterprise in China and America.* Ed. John K. Fairbank. Harvard University Press, 1974. p254.
[4] Miller, Stuart Creighton. "Ends and Means." *The Missionary Enterprise in China and America.* Ed. John K. Fairbank. Harvard University Press, 1974. p256.
[5] M. Searle Bates. *Gleanings: The Protestant Endeavor in Chinese Society, 1890-1950.* p. 50.
[6] Miller, Stuart Creighton. "Ends and Means." *The Missionary Enterprise in China and America.* Ed. John K. Fairbank. Harvard University Press, 1974. p274.
[7] Miller, Stuart Creighton. "Ends and Means." *The Missionary Enterprise in China and America.* Ed. John K. Fairbank. Harvard University Press, 1974. p275.
[8] *San Francisco Call*, June 20, 1900.
[9] Miller, Stuart Creighton. "Ends and Means." *The Missionary Enterprise in China and America.* Ed. John K. Fairbank. Harvard University Press, 1974. p275.

Chapter 2

An Examination of Current Trends in China

"If you want to know what China will be like in the future, you have to consider the future of Christianity in China."

—*Chinese House Church leader,* The Economist

A Rainy Taxi Ride

I have ridden in a lot of Chinese taxis in my years of work and life in China. Truly, I have ridden in thousands and thousands of taxis. I have been in big taxis, small taxis, the now banned 'bread loaf' taxis of Tianjin that I miss so much, red taxis, yellow taxis…so many taxis. But there is one taxi ride that is the most memorable of all.

In December 2002, I was back in China for the first time since my family and I had returned from the U.S. I was sharing the taxi ride with a fellow American friend whom I had gotten to know while we lived in Tianjin. As we traveled together through the bustling streets in China, I told her about all the ways we were beginning to serve the rapid growth and development of the Church in China. I talked excitedly about the Bible Training Center we had been asked to open, and I told her about our journey to bring several thousand books from Hong Kong to fill the library. The collection of books included the translated works of Spurgeon, R. C. Sproul, and a host of others. As we zipped through the city of Tianjin on a wet, rainy winter afternoon, I talked of the Bibles that are now being printed in China; I shared my plans of doing Bible Distribution Events out in rural and remote areas, where they are desperately clamoring for Bibles.

As I continued talking, paragraph after paragraph, my friend interrupted me, mid-sentence. "Mike," she said, "Wait. Stop. All of this sounds exciting, but none of it is allowed today, is it? I assumed all of this would not have been possible!" With great joy, I explained that it is not only possible, but we had been invited to participate in these activities.

Later that day, as I reflected on our conversation, two key thoughts struck me: clearly, the changes taking place in China were coming fast—really fast. My friend had committed her entire life to the ministry in China, even parting with family and friends for the sake of the believers there; her unawareness of the changes within China were evidence of how fast they had truly taken place. She belonged to a generation of Christian workers who were initially trained to view China as if a 'security bubble' was built around them, so it is tremendously significant for that security to be unnecessary. (As a side note, it is also noteworthy to think that this 'security bubble' may actually keep Westerners in China from seeing all the changes around them.) Further, I realized that if I truly intended to stay current with the best ways to serve

China and the Chinese people, then I had better be willing to commit my time to regularly monitoring and analyzing these changes.

I'm happy to report that in the time between the 1st and 2nd Editions of this book, there are many organizations that have realized both the non-necessity of the 'security bubble' and also the opportunity to work more openly in China. The openness takes on several forms, whether by getting to know Government officials that oversee the area they'd like to work or by changing their approach to how they communicate to others about what they are doing in China. In my opinion, these are all very good developments.

Monumental Shift

On December 19th, 2007, China's President, Hu Jintao, presented a speech that headlines some of the changes taking place in China. Hu delivered the speech in Beijing; he had overseen the Chinese Communist Party (CCP) Central Committee Political Bureau second collective study on contemporary world religion and China's religious situation. This was the first time the Party Central Committee Political Bureau organized a collective study of religion, and it was also the first time that the top person in the Party spoke officially about religion, devoting his entire speech to the topic.

The collective study and the resulting speech surprised us. We've seen the 'writing on the wall,' as the intentions of the Chinese Federal Government have been unveiled. We began to see a road map unfold with the development of the Department of Christian Studies departments at many of China's top universities at the start of the 21st Century. This was closely followed by the now famous story found in David Aikman's book, *Jesus in Beijing*,[1] published in 2003.

Mr. Aikman begins his book by recalling a speech by a Chinese scholar specializing in the study of religion for China's premier academic research institute, the Chinese Academy of Social Sciences. In the speech, the scholar presented the factors which accounted for the pre-eminence of the West all over the world. He and his team studied everything from the historical, political, economic and cultural perspective. After finding that the West's preeminence did not come from military might, or from a better economic or political system, they were left with only one conclusion. "But in the past twenty years, we have realized that the heart of your culture is your religion: Christianity. That is why the West has been so powerful. That Christian moral foundation of social and cultural life made possible the emergence of capitalism and then the successful transition to democratic politics. We don't have any doubt about this," said the researcher.

Dr. Aikman also quoted the former President of China, Jiang Zemin. As Zemin was leaving his role as President, someone asked him this question: "If you could make one decree that you knew would be obeyed in China, what would it be?" With a broad smile on his face, President Jiang answered, "I would make Christianity the official religion of China." This information clearly indicated that the Chinese Government had developed an intense interest in utilizing that which had made the West so powerful; they were ready to use that force in their quest for social stability and growing power on the World stage.

We began to hear stories of local Religious Affair Bureaus (RAB) in major cities taking action to make life easier for people of faith. Most recently, we've heard repeated stories of American pastors and lay leaders recruited to teach Christian ethics in government and education circles in China. Fenggang Yang, a Chinese national and now a Purdue University sociology professor, states, "China's increasing global role is undisputed in economics and politics, but religious changes—China's ongoing transition from a secular state to a religious state is often overlooked in the West."[2] Professor Yang is a member of the religious and Asian studies programs in Purdue's College of Liberal Arts, and he directs a three-year project focused on training Chinese scholars to study religion and improve Americans' understanding of religious issues in China.

To me, President Hu's speech seems to be 'the next step' in the evolution of the Chinese Government's perspective on people of faith in China. In the speech, President Hu made a couple of key comments. He mentioned the positive role that religious believers have in promoting economic and social development, which is similar to the early 20th Century thought that the Protestant ethic, a code of morals based on the principles of thrift, discipline, hard work, and individualism, is closely tied to the spirit of capitalism. He also mentioned in the speech that at all levels of Chinese Government, they are realizing that religious beliefs are going to be a constant in Chinese society for the foreseeable future, so the government must change to meet their needs. In addition, Hu mentioned that together with people of faith, the Chinese Government wanted to cooperate to make a patriotic citizenry, have mutual respect in belief among the Chinese people, and promote social harmony. Religion in Chinese society now plays a necessary and constructive role.

Also very notable is the final comment of President Hu's speech, in which he stressed the training and promotion of religious professionals, saying the CPC would help and support religious groups to improve self-governance, and they would voice the opinions of its followers and protect their legal rights and interests. The tone of his comment indicates that we must view this as a complaint against the current state of affairs within the RAB workers' realm of influence.

In the 1st edition of this book, published in 2008 not long after this speech was delivered, I made a few notes about the speech, which are as important now as they were then for those of us watching the development of religious affairs in China. First, his instruction was authoritative and intended for the government bureaucracy nationwide. We also note that religion in China under Communism is set in a neutral setting for the first time, and it does not have to bear the burden of history or be cast in suspicious and negative roles. The perspectives which government leaders have traditionally held regarding religion were not mentioned in Hu's speech. (In China, what is not said is often more important than what is said.)

For those of us who are either sending people into China or working together with Chinese nationals, there is another "first" in this speech. This is the first time that the Chinese government brought up the topic of religion, without simultaneously warning about the dangers of Western infiltration and subversive activities. In the past, any religious speech from a Chinese Government official carried an admonition to the Chinese people: be careful, because religion will always have ties to Western Imperialists who want nothing more than to take over China. Finally, since the official religious organs (like the Three Self Patriotic Movement, or TSPM) were not highlighted in this speech, this indicates that the Chinese Federal Government knows what we know: the registered church bodies, like the TSPM, are decreasing in influence, and as long as social stability can be maintained, the government is willing to allow Chinese Christians to live within the Chinese Socialist society with an increasing amount of autonomy.

I have a perfect example of the shrinking influence of the TSPM from my work in China. As many of you know, our organization works with TSPM officials in the provinces where we do our projects. We developed these relationships initially through a good friend of mine who is a registered church pastor in China. My pastor friend, whose English name is Joel, is required twice a year to attend national TSPM pastor meetings in Shanghai. The purpose of these meetings is to train and equip the pastors of the TSPM nationwide. Joel often tells me that during these meetings, most pastors are in attendance, but the content of the meetings is often brushed aside by those in attendance. After meeting their requirement of attendance, these pastors then go back to their local pastorate and continue their ministry without regard for what the National leadership may be requiring of them. Joel recently told me that he 'wouldn't be surprised if the TSPM is completely defunct by the year 2020.'

We continue to hear the stories of the massive growth of the Church in China. Millions of Chinese Christians, many of who are from rural areas, have come to know Christ. Some China analysts have called it 'the greatest evangelical movement the world has ever seen.' Our estimates indicate that there are now over 70 million Christians, and the Christian Church in China is growing at a rate of 6% a year. In my own work in China, I am in contact with rural Chinese pastors who baptize 1,000 new believers a year. As Westerners, we are trying to put the pieces together in our understanding, attempting to reconcile the large growth of the church in China, and working to comprehend the government's view of people of faith. I've found a few key pieces to help us in our examination of current trends.

Developing Rule of Law

According to Article 36 in the Constitution of the People's Republic of China (PRC), "....citizens of the PRC enjoy freedom of religious belief. No state organ, public organization, or individuals may compel citizens to believe in, or not to believe in, any religion." This guarantees Chinese citizens the opportunity to worship God freely.

However, the government seeks, in varying degrees from province to province, to monitor religious practice to government-sanctioned organizations and registered places of worship, and to oversee the growth and scope of the activity of religious groups, all in an effort to prevent the rise of competing possible sources of authority outside of the control of the government. This much is clear: the Communist Party in China will not tolerate threats to its existence and will use the law at times to quash perceived threats. This causes some misunderstanding among Westerners, who are looking from the outside in; it underscores one of the main difficulties of religious affairs in China and the situation of Christianity in China: the lack of 'rule of law' in China.

Generally defined, rule of law states that governmental authorities must make decisions based on the application of known principles or laws, without using personal discretion. In other words, when laws are in the books, authorities must use them 100% of the time, in a consistent manner, to determine whether someone has broken those laws. In order for a government to govern, it may only use the powers granted by certain laws (i.e. constitutional laws).

In China, the national government has drafted a number of laws that relate to religious affairs in China, and provincial and local officials have the ability to administer those laws. Many times, people in authority administer those laws differently, in different places. Traditionally, China has lacked a rule of law culture, in which law was held in high esteem. It has only been in the last fifty years that they've literally rebuilt their legal system; creating a culture of legality takes even longer. To note the difficulty of the task is not to apologize for the failures of the system or to absolve China's leaders of responsibility when they abuse their power. Ultimately, this is a power issue. In the absence of genuine multiparty democracy, implementation of rule of law in China depends on the voluntary compliance of the Party; it requires the Party to abide by the law, even though it may jeopardize the Party's ability to continue to rule.

Allow me to give you a practical example of why rule of law is important for our understanding of China. Even with all of the improvements within the last thirty years, there are still rural public security bureau officials who do not yet have the oversight structure to even administer Article 36. A recent article in *Christianity Today* told of a group of lawyers in Beijing who started an organization called the Human Rights Protection Movement (HRPM).[3] These lawyers have become the official legal counsel for a Church alliance of smaller, rural churches. They help rural church leaders know their rights under the law, and they educate rural public security officials to know how far they can go. The article unveiled a wonderful story of the fruits of their efforts.

A rural church pastor was worried about the poverty levels striking his area, so he set up a sewing school in the home of a local Christian. Every day, the school opened with Bible Study, singing, and prayer. After he had established the school, local police invaded to search for evidence that the school was an illegal church. The pastor, trained by HRPM lawyers regarding his legal rights, told the police to stop. "What you are doing is illegal. I am calling my legal counsel in Beijing!" The pastor called HRPM in Beijing, and he told the police officers, "My legal counsel says you need a search warrant with an official red seal. Where is it?"

Unwilling to provoke Beijing-level attention, the policeman gruffly shouted, "We don't have a search warrant, but we will get one. You stay here until I get back!"

To underscore the importance of rule of law, the Criminal Law in China prohibits this type of activity by law enforcement officials. The Law states that government officials who deprive citizens of religious freedom may, in serious cases, be sentenced to up to two years in prison; however, there have been no documented cases of punished officials under this statute.

The people in the Chinese culture have relied heavily on personal connections to circumvent the law, and they have historically believed morality trumps law, so each one of these changes is a fairly major development. China also tends to give wide discretion to decision makers, so it is unrealistic and unfair for Westerners to expect China to be equivalent with the West. We should avoid the tendency to focus exclusively on violations of human rights or to compare China's legal system to an idealized version in more developed countries. We must recognize and applaud the remarkable progress that has taken place in China's legal system in the last twenty-five years.

For those of us looking at China from the outside, we definitely see something different than what we are accustomed to, and we do not understand the context of Christianity in China. We see individual authorities interpreting the laws differently. The National Government in China has given legal ability to provincial and local authorities, enabling them to determine what a law states and how it should be administered. This causes problems in China, because no standard exists from which the whole of the country can work. So, when we foreigners hear about a persecution story in China, it is easy for us to think initially that this type of persecution must occur throughout the whole country. This simply isn't true. In some areas of China, house churches operate in legal standing from their cities' municipalities, but in other areas, there is certain persecution. The situation is unique to each location, and negative stereotypes of China are false as well as damaging to God's overall work in China.

Regarding this confusion, I continue to encourage and pray for the development of China. Ned Graham, the President of East Gates Ministries and the son of evangelist Billy Graham, testified before the United States Senate Committee on Finance in March 2000. His testimony was important for my own understanding of the challenges that China faces. In his testimony, he addressed the absence of rule of law in China, and he suggested some actions China could take to effectively improve this situation. Here's what Ned wrote: "A worthy goal in the area of religious freedom would be to encourage China to fully define and publish all policies, laws and rules governing religion, from the governmental level, all the way down to the township level. China can be encouraged to publish and clarify all internal directives concerning Article 36 of its Constitution. China should also clarify (by written rule) exactly how it expects all officials (whether it is the State Religious Affairs Administration, the Public Security Bureau or local village officials) to interpret and implement these religious policies. It would also be helpful if there was either a set penalty for officials who violated these religious policies, or a procedure for forcing their accountability and providing redress for individuals whose rights are violated."[4]

The Chinese Government recognizes the importance of the development of rule of law in China as well. A recent article in the *Washington Post* exclaimed, "A momentous struggle is underway in China between a ruling party that sees the law as an instrument of control and a society that increasingly believes it should be used for something else: a check on the power of government officials and a guardian of individual rights. How this conflict unfolds could transform the country's authoritarian political system." Governmental officials are aware of this need to govern more responsibly. At their annual planning session in September 2004, National Government leaders said that "the life and death of the party" rests on "improving governance."[5]

As of the end of 2011, China continues to make progress in the development of rule of law. Since 1978 when China began reforms, they have passed 450 new laws, 650 administrative regulations and 7,500 local regulations. Many times, public consultations have taken place on a number of these new laws, including the 2008 Contract Law. Chinese Governmental Officials have been working with the United Nations Development Program (UNDP) to continue the process of becoming a Rule of Law state. UNDP has been working with the National People's Congress while a basic legal infrastructure is being established. UNDP is also helping to standardize provincial and national law-making processes. By the veracity of activity within Chinese leadership in 2011, it seems like leaders in China want to get serious about Rule of Law. In 2011 alone, there was a Politburo study session on Rule of Law, a symposium for leading cadres from provincial governments and ministries and a May 30th Politburo meeting on strengthening and promoting innovation in governance. These meetings reflect the seriousness with which the nation's leaders are confronting the challenge of rising social tension. They've also acknowledged the many problems in governance, both in theory and practice, that contribute to the stress in Chinese society.

Registration of Religious Activities

In my opinion, one of the hardest things for Christians in the West to 'wrap our minds around' regarding Christianity in China is the notion of needing to get approval, or having to register. Registration of religious activities and organizations is a reality in China today. The Chinese Government has set guidelines and boundaries around what are acceptable religious conduct and activities in China. There is no getting around this fact, but this reality irritates us Westerners to no end. In this section, I give you a basic look at this topic. In Chapter 5, I examine this topic in much more detail.

As citizens of Western culture, we view freedom of religion and belief, for individuals and groups, as a guarantee from government. Many consider this freedom to be a fundamental human right. Freedom of religion must include the freedom to practice no religion as well as the belief that there exists no deity. Accordingly, in China, government has always had some regulatory measures over religious activities. But through the lens of dynastic succession throughout Chinese history, we find Emperors of China who alone had the 'Mandate of Heaven' to rule China. With this Mandate, they had Heaven's blessing to rule China, and these Emperors were often called 'the Son of Heaven.'

Likewise, if they ruled immorally, they could lose the Mandate, and several dynasties, such as the Han (206 B.C. to

220 A.D), went to great lengths to preserve the Mandate. With this Mandate, the Emperor was the representative to God for the Chinese people, and only he had the right to dictate the religious affairs of the Chinese people. This mindset, albeit in a different context, continues in some regard with the present day rulers of China. Some have said that Chinese history is simply a series of Chinese Dynasties, and if we are to be a blessing to the Chinese people today, we need to work within the boundaries set by the current dynasty.

Because the Chinese situation is so different from the West, the following analogy may aid in our understanding. Imagine a huge, domed stadium that holds 100,000 professional soccer fields. This domed stadium would be one of the only man-made structures one can see from a spacecraft, looking down at the earth from outer space. The government's position on religious affairs is similar to that huge dome; there's a lot you can do in there. Within the dome, they are printing Bibles in large quantities; they allow 55,000 Christian Churches to operate openly and legally. And today, even unregistered urban churches operate with relative freedom. Scores of Western Christians are permitted to come and work together with the Church in China on a varied number of projects. The dome in China is an immense place where they're allowing great things to happen. Hundreds of thousands of Chinese have found Christ under the dome.

In China, you could say, 'It's all good under the dome,' but what happens if you go outside the dome? The Chinese Government has created the environment where Chinese Christians are arrested for printing Bibles, for meeting in unregistered places, etc. To leave the dome is to do so at your own risk. This analogy is important for our understanding of China. Within the sphere of what's allowed, we have permission to bless the Chinese people in many ways. This is their country, and the governmental authorities feel it is their 'right' to put controls on religious affairs.

Printing Bibles in China

Since 1988, the Amity Printing Company has been printing Bibles in Nanjing, China. Last year alone, they printed over 7 million Bibles for the Chinese Church. Amity Printing is a joint venture between the Amity Foundation and the United Bible Societies (UBS). Amity Foundation is a Chinese-run, social service, non-profit organization, and UBS is the world fellowship for many of the worldwide Bible Societies, such as the American Bible Society, Scottish Bible Society, etc. Their purpose is to achieve the widest possible effective and meaningful distribution of the Holy Scriptures, and they also seek to help people interact with the Word of God.

The UBS responsibility at Amity Press is to raise the money for the paper on which the Bibles are printed, which helps minimize the cost of each Bible. The China Christian Council (on behalf of Amity Foundation) must apply for approval to print a certain amount of Bibles at one time. This same application is required to print any book in Nanjing. So, for example, if they wanted to print 700,000 Bibles, they fill out the paperwork to print that many Bibles, and then they receive approval.

Interestingly, there is no limit to the number of completed or approved applications. If the church needs seven million Bibles, they could get approval for that many. Once the Bibles are printed, they travel by railcar to seventy distribution points, where registered church Bible outlets and bookstores sell them. Amity Press has the capacity to print twelve million Bibles a year, and in 2008, they built a 10-acre printing facility that will have the capability to print one million new Bibles every month. Amity Press prints a wide variety of Bibles, including study Bibles, pocket Bibles, large print Bibles, and a variety of diglot versions with Chinese/English and Chinese/English/Hebrew/Greek.

There have been many misconceptions of the Amity Bibles, although I am frankly unsure of where these misconceptions originated. I've heard that the Amity Press Bibles are not complete Bibles, and they intentionally leave out the book of Revelation. This is not true. If UBS is going to participate in printing Bibles in China, they will be quality Bibles!

Chinese University Department of Christian Studies

In Beijing, Tianjin, Shanghai, Guangzhou, and other cities, you'll find universities with Departments of Christians and/or Religious Studies. These departments, which began just a few years ago, have spread rapidly and have been a catalyst for revision of government policy on Chinese Christians. They are significant, at least partially because China's universities have long been a key area of control for the Communist Party. They have, however, given pastors and graduates with a Master of Divinity in the West another chance to work transparently in China. Western Biblical scholars and university professors have noted the significance of these programs.

David L. Jeffrey, Vice President of Baylor University, observed one of these programs in action. He reported, "The level of sophistication of contemporary religious studies in China is high, particularly for the scholarly appreciation of the remarkable history and steadily evolving contemporary role of Christian thought in Chinese intellectual life."[6]

I agree with the significance of the advent of these Departments, especially from the standpoint of the Chinese Government's evolving thought on the Christian influence in China. Through speeches from government leaders over the last several years, and through the actions of loosening religious policy, governmental attitudes toward Christians are changing.

Paolo Santangelo, professor of Chinese History at the University of Naples, agrees. "Fifteen years ago, few experts of modern China would dare to think that theological studies would be recognized as a research field within the academic world and in Chinese society. The 'discovery' of theology gives an idea of the tremendous changes done in China in recent times."[7]

One may ask how these departments developed and what type of spiritual climate led to their advancement. Throughout the last twenty-five years, Chinese academicians in the fields of literature, history, philosophy and the social sciences have attempted to rebuild their theoretical foundation in a more open context. Many Chinese professors of philosophy, foreign languages, literature, art, history and social sciences have taken an interest in Christianity as an academic subject of research. Within this group of professors, some have come to faith in Christ. In China, this group is commonly known as "Cultural Christians." They do not attend or identify with any church, but their goal is to make Christianity a visible force as China searches for a new intellectual order in the 21st century. They promote Christian ideas and values in the Chinese academic context. Their influence in these Chinese universities has grown, and the emergence of these Departments of Christian Studies is the natural outpouring of their efforts.

One of the IICS professors, who teaches Biblical Studies in a secular Shanghai university, reports that his Chinese colleague, the Director of the department, has high hopes to develop this department into a national center for biblical studies. He has already formed a small library, and he has big plans for this department. This causes me to stop and ask: If the Chinese Government intends to strongly persecute Christians, why do they allow these departments to exist? They are breeding grounds for the next generation of great Christian thinkers and leaders in China. From them will come the next generation of Christian scholars, writers, and missions leaders. Just recently, I've personally talked with Western pastors who have also been asked to teach Christian Ethics at the Central Party School in Beijing, the highest institution in China to train high-ranking officials within the Communist Party.

Of course, we think we can answer our own question; time and time again, we see trends indicating that policy-makers in China see Christians as a benefit to society. Miikka Ruokanen, Professor of Systematic Theology at the University of Helsinki, takes this perspective: "In modern China, Christian faith is no longer a controversial choice. Christianity, along with other religions, has gained some public sphere and recognition in recent years."[8]

Creative New Ministry Opportunities

There are several examples of Westerners who saw a need in China and found a way to meet that need. Their stories illustrate how this open approach to ministry can produce effective results.

One of my favorite organizations to introduce people to when I'm taking a group through China is Bao Jia Yin, or GoodNewsinChina.com. Bao Jia Yin is the brainchild of my friend, Gary Hopwood. Gary, a former international senior manager with UPS, came to China after many years of success in the business world. Having the intention of trying to make a difference in China, Gary came initially to China to do Chinese language study in Tianjin. After his China arrival, Gary invested in a Chinese publishing company and was contacted by a consulting company who asked him to lead a team that would study the Chinese market for a large faith-based distributor. Knowing his interest in publishing and his vast experience in distribution with UPS, the consulting company thought Gary would be perfect to lead the team. In the process of doing this study, two significant things happened. First, the large distributor was no longer interested in doing business in the Chinese market, but Gary had learned quite a bit about the market and the titles that would available in China. In particular, Gary started to find out that there were many publication companies in China that were legally printing Christian books of various topics.

To print any book in China, you must receive an ISBN number from the provincial Press and Publication Bureau in your area. Over the last 20 years, many different printing presses have received approval to print Christian books, mostly to sell those books in their local province. During the research phase, Gary saw a fundamental problem and an opportunity to make a difference. The problem was that no one in Beijing, for example, knew that a Kunming printing press (1700 miles away) had printed a translated volume of John Stott's *Understanding the Bible*. There was no central catalog of all Christian books legally printed in China and therefore, no way for people throughout China to know what was available. So the opportunity that Gary realized came in the form of a question: What if we could gather all the Christian books that are legally available in China in one warehouse? Furthermore, what if then we could set up an online and phone order store to make these titles available to any person in China and ship them to any address in China?

Figuring out the answers to those questions resulted in Bao Jia Yin, located in Beijing. Bao Jia Yin now has over 450 titles in Chinese that come from over 30 different publishers. The 10 staff members really make the organization work like a well-oiled machine. Once an order is placed, it can be shipped to any address in China. Each order, wrapped in a clear plastic wrap to make sure authorities in China have no questions about the contents of the package, are shipped for only 5 quai, which is about 80¢, regardless of the quantity of books ordered. Bao Jia Yin has two websites, one in Chinese (BaoJiaYin.com) and one in English (goodnewsinchina.com). The English website has a very good interface, where the books are divided into 18 categories, such as Biography, Business Training, Dating and Marriage, Evangelism/

Apologetics, Leadership Development, New Believer, Theology, and Parenting. Among the 450 plus titles, there are quite a few good titles and books I didn't even know where available in Chinese: Everything from *What Wives Wish their Husbands knew about Marriage* by Dr. James Dobson to *The Cost of Discipleship* by Dietrich Bonhoeffer to *Running with the Giants* by John Maxwell.

This is but one example of a Westerner who came to China to be a blessing to China. The environment in China is such that if you have an idea on your heart, you probably can find a way to do it.

Emerging Election Process throughout China

When we think about China, we don't think of it as a place for democratic elections. But slowly and consistently, the Chinese Government is giving a voice to rural villagers. Many watchers of the election process refer to this village election as the world's largest grassroots democratic education process. The Chinese Government initiated direct village elections in 1988, to help maintain social and political order in the context of rapid economic reforms. Today, village elections occur in about 650,000 villages across China, reaching 75 percent of the nation's 1.3 billion people. Many of these elections have garnered the attention of others, like former U.S. President Jimmy Carter, who has sent election monitors from his Carter Center.

The widespread popularity of these elections led to a revision in Chinese law to include procedures that guarantee electoral openness, fairness, and competitiveness. The changes forbid local Communist Party committees from intervening in the nomination phase, and they encouraged more elected village officials to challenge party control within the villages. While it is clear that China's rural villages are seeing mixed results as to the success of these elections, it is important to note that they are changing the local landscape and thinking about how officials come into office. In many areas, successful village elections also prompted experiments of public election of township leaders—the next highest level of government in three provinces.

Less Ability to Control the Information Sector

Through the 1980's and early 1990's, the Chinese Government tried to maintain a grip on the information sector and repeatedly launched campaigns against liberalization tendencies in the mass media. But these efforts have failed miserably. Although the government has maintained relatively strict controls on television and radio networks, it has effectively ceded control of much of the print media to the private sector. Today, China has an efficient, privately controlled network of publishing companies, printing facilities, and retail distributors.

In addition, the introduction of new information technology, including electronic mail, fax machines, satellite television transmission and video CD and DVD players has further reduced the state's capacity for social control. The one area where the local Government is struggling to release is certain social media and information websites that are blocked in China. Websites like Facebook and Twitter, which were blocked after the 2009 Summer riots in Xinjiang province, have yet to be reinstated. The blockage however is easily circumvented through several means. All of this has led to new opportunities, not only for Bible printing, but also for Christian radio and television programming.

New Chinese-Led Initiatives are 'Outside the Box'

I have seen an increasing number of Chinese Christians using the new liberalization to further God's kingdom in China. Those Chinese Christians, with a heart to see the advancement of God's good news, have found new ways to serve in China. A friend of our ministry, who is a registered church pastor, has a deep heart for Christian counseling. He had a vision to provide a nationwide Christian counseling center, for which there was no paradigm. Knowing that he would need proper training for his center, he moved to Canada and obtained a master's degree in Christian counseling from a prestigious seminary. He returned to China, and he operates a Christian counseling center with a walk-in service and three nationwide crisis counseling hotlines. While the hotlines are open, trained counselors field the calls. He reports that they receive phone calls from people who are in crisis in all corners of China. They counsel them from a Christian perspective, and they introduce them to the only One who can truly give them peace.

I have found another example of this trend in Chengdu, where I met with a Chinese Christian who has recognized the immense needs of a community north of his city. He has started a non-profit organization to help meet the needs of the poor in this village area. His organization provides many services, like English, job training, after-school programs, medical assistance, and basic needs like clothes, backpacks and shoes for school children. Programs such as this one are so encouraging because they are Chinese-led and operated. It is another step toward the Chinese Church's complete self-sufficiency.

The Church in China Today

Most Westerners want to define the Church in China in black and white terms, because we like when things are clear and concise. We tend to think that Chinese Christians participate in either the registered church or the unregistered (house) church.

In reality, four different church groups operate in China, and we must have a careful understanding of these groups in order to value the Church in China.

Registered Churches

This group is often called the 'government church' by some Westerners since they must register with a religious affairs division of the government in order to operate. A religious affairs body, called the State Administration of Religious Affairs (SARA), is a national governmental department that oversees religious affairs in China. SARA is under the authority of the State Council. The State Council is the highest executive organ of State power, as well as the highest organ of State administration. The Chinese Government has a division of the State Council called the United Front Works Department (UFWD), and SARA operates in China through the UFWD.

On both a national and local level, SARA has five main divisions, one for each of the five state-sponsored religions: Protestantism, Catholicism, Islam, Buddhism, and Daoism. In this system, under the Protestant SARA division, there are two main organs that oversee and execute Protestant activities in China. The first is the Three-Self Patriotic Movement (TSPM), and the second is the China Christian Council (CCC). These two organizations are somewhat similar in function, but they also have their differences. To summarize their differences, the TSPM serves to help the government implement its religious policies among Christian believers, and they regulate foreign Christians' or organizations' involvement in Christian work in China. The CCC assists the local churches in their daily operations. In addition to Sunday morning worship services and Sunday School, the CCC also oversees the 18 seminaries in China and conducts a certain amount of public relations with overseas Chinese and foreign Christian visitors. Within this framework, the SARA administers the Protestant Church in China.

Often misrepresented and mischaracterized in the West, most of these churches are urban, with trained professional clergy and church buildings. Since 1979, they have been the backbone of the nationwide movement to recover old church buildings, open seminaries and Bible schools, publish Bibles and literature, and sponsor public works of compassion. Largely Evangelistic and broadly Orthodox at the local level, these churches are the 'public face' of Christianity in China. They offer Chinese people the opportunity to go to a church building on Sunday mornings, to allow their children to receive teaching in Sunday school classes, which are also very common.

The openness of these churches presents a unique situation, because they have the freedom to operate openly and legally in China. In my interviews and the time I have spent with the younger generations of registered church leaders, they are optimizing their opportunity to minister more openly. The pastors can extend invitations to accept Christ from the pulpit every week. They offer open-air evangelism, develop widespread children's Sunday school classes and lay leader training; these are only a few of the things that these pastors can do today in China. Church bookstores reside at almost all of the 55,000 registered church buildings in China, so they are the main locations for purchasing a Bible.

Meeting Point Churches

These churches often meet in homes or other non-church structures. They are legally registered with the government, but lay elders lead them rather than professionally trained clergy. Many times, those who participate in meeting point churches do not have a registered church building in their area, but they also have no issues with the registration process. Amongst those participants whom I've talked to, they report that there are no problems with government officials trying to control their activities, and they view registration as a positive requirement. They have access to all CCC Publishing material, but they also have contacts with the unregistered Church.

Unregistered House Church

Most of these church groups meet in apartments, and they tend to be urban, led by seasoned Christians who have a legacy of grievances with the government or the Three-Self Patriotic Movement, dating back to the 1950's. These church groups are often part of a 'network' of other unregistered churches, and these networks frequently share training resources. Many urban participants also attend registered church activities, and they regularly utilize the registered church as their source for good Bibles. Most of the persecution resulting from the lack of 'rule of law' in China happens to those who are leaders in the unregistered churches. Mostly, though, the local governments tolerate these groups. Their meetings are half-kept secrets.

In some areas of China, Christian believers in the official registered churches and unofficial unregistered churches live alongside one another without any problems. Some Christians are involved in both registered and house churches; others work together with believers from the other group. I continually hear stories of people who may attend a registered church service on Sunday morning, and then during the week they participate in an unregistered church Bible Study. I know of several unregistered church pastors' sons attending TSPM seminaries. Also, many urban unregistered church members use the registered church bookstores as a reliable source for Bibles.

While there are exemptions throughout the country, the unregistered House Church in Beijing has to be the most current and the most notable exception. In this Second Edition, I'm dedicating a full chapter to Beijing's Unregistered Churches, which you'll find in chapter 5.

Rural Christian Groups

This church group is the most difficult to characterize, even though it is the largest. Located in villages and in the countryside, they are far away from organized churches in cities or towns. Although most of them are not registered, their meetings are publicly known. Church registration is a "city" concept, and it has little meaning for the rural groups.

It is the fastest growing segment of the church in China, and it presents the most concern because of its lack of resources and training in remote areas of China. Since this community of Chinese Christians gather in remote locations, this is also the church group that is most vulnerable to false teaching and heresy. Repeatedly, Church and seminary leaders in the cities have told us of the needs in the rural areas for lay and pastoral training, theological education, and Bibles. They've also told us of how they've baptized 1000 new believers in the last year and we hear these same types of numbers throughout rural China.

China's Cultural Christians: A Growing "Third Wave" Church

One of the most interesting trends happening within Chinese Christianity is the emergence of the 'Third Wave' Church, signifying a separate movement from the registered and unregistered church movements. Largely urban in development, they are well-educated professionals: bankers, doctors, professors, entrepreneurs, or people working for multinational corporations. Also called China's 'Cultural Christians,' they generally are non-baptized, literate in Christian studies, and adhere to Christian principles and theology in their own lives, morality, and ethics. They have mostly chosen not to worship in Church because of the lack of connection with the registered and unregistered churches. Given their elite status in Chinese urban society, they have a great opportunity and capacity to impact high levels of society.

Many of these intellectuals have taken an interest in Christianity as an academic subject of research, especially among those in academia. The emergence of Christian or Religious Studies Departments in most of China's large universities is the product of their interest in the study of Christianity as a foundation for society.

Many Chinese professors of philosophy, social sciences, literature, foreign languages, art, and history have taken an interest in Christianity as an academic subject of research. Their goal is to make Christianity a visible force in China's search for a new social and intellectual order in the 21st century. They are able to accomplish this goal through their positions in business, academia or the government. Many of these Cultural Christians have been on a long journey from an atheistic theory to Christian Theology. Seeing Christianity as a solution to the ills of Chinese society, they have set a primary goal to put Christianity on the front stage of contemporary Chinese intellectual development. To understand their intellectual inquiry is to feel the pain and anxiety of contemporary Chinese intellectuals, as they seek to fill an ideological vacuum and shape China's social, spiritual and moral order for the future.

[1] Aikman, David. *Jesus in Beijing*: How Christianity Is Transforming China and Changing the Global Balance of Power. Washington, D.C. Regnery Publishing. 2003.
[2] Perdue University. "Chinese religious trends attracting scholars' attention." [Online] May 27, 2005. < http://news.uns.purdue.edu/html4ever/2005/050527.Yang.religion. html>.
[3] Tony Carnes, "China's New Legal Eagles," *Christianity Today*, September 2006.
[4] Testimony of Nelson E. Graham, President, East Gates International, Before the Senate Committee on Finance. US-China Trade Relations and the Impact on Religious Activity in the PRC. March 23, 2000.
[5] Kahn, Joseph. "China's 'Haves' Stir the 'Have Nots' to Violence." **New York Times**, Dec. 31, 2004.
[6] Ed. Yang Huilin and Daniel H. N. YEUNG. Sino Christian Studies in China. Cambridge Scholars Press. 2006.
[7] Ed. Yang Huilin and Daniel H. N. YEUNG. Sino Christian Studies in China. Cambridge Scholars Press. 2006.
[8] Ed. Yang Huilin and Daniel H. N. YEUNG. Sino Christian Studies in China. Cambridge Scholars Press. 2006.

Chapter 3

East and West— an Insider's Look at Modern Day Chinese

"If there are fifteen Government regulations out there, you foreigners should follow all of them, since you are guests in this country. However, we Chinese might choose twelve of them that we follow carefully, but three of them we'll challenge, and try to get our Government to reconsider. If you foreigners challenge the Government, you force us to choose between loyalty to our Government or to a foreign group. Because of the history of foreign Christians in China, it is better if you stay here long term, building relationships, supporting

and encouraging us as friends, as we, the Chinese, lead the way for change in China."
—A Senior Chinese Church Pastor, speaking recently to a group of Westerners

Imagine this situation...

As you finish a phone call with a friend, you say, "Okay, Bill. No, I'm not sure what to do about those Angolans either! They treat us like they know best! We'll talk more about this at next Wednesday's Elder meeting. Thanks for your call."

As you hang up the phone, you cannot shake the nagging feeling you have felt since the missionaries from the African country of Angola came to town. Sitting on your couch, searching for solutions, you review in your mind all that has happened in the last year with the Angolans. They obviously came to your town excited about their call as missionaries to America, and they have a deep heart to reach unsaved Americans with the Gospel of Jesus Christ. They were trained, equipped, and commissioned by a very respectable African missions organization. But since they came from a Portuguese-speaking country, their English was poor; they hadn't studied any English before coming here. They obviously didn't understand American culture either, and you have always clearly understood that they consider their own culture to be superior to yours.

When the Angolans arrived in your town, they chose your church as their base of operations, because they said, "God told us your church should be our base." Shortly after arriving, they started using your church for a variety of outreach and evangelistic programs, even though you and many others at your church felt the programs were ineffective and didn't meet the needs of the intended American audience.

As the Elder over the missions effort at your church, you've taken much of the heat for this situation. First, you listened to criticism from the congregation, many of whom simply wanted the Angolans to leave. Many people felt uncomfortable around them, since they were from a different country and culture.

But then, you received visits from U.S. Government officials, including the Department of Homeland Security and Immigration and Naturalization Department, asking questions about these foreigners. They wanted to know: Why were they here? Was your church sponsoring them or supporting them financially at all? The officials have closely followed a terror organization with ties in Angola. Of course, you've told all officials that the Church has not sponsored these Angolans and you do not have any official ties with them. But on more than one Sunday service, you've noticed men with sunglasses sitting in the back of the sanctuary; they were obviously not a part of the Church.

As you've discerned this situation, there are several reasons for their ineffectiveness of the Angolans. Clearly, they do not understand Americans, and their limited use of our language has not helped them grow in their understanding. As you've tried to offer suggestions, they've been very unwilling to listen to your ideas, as if they are really the ones who know best. Sometimes they have cooperated with you and your church, but only to the extent that benefited their missionary cause. After all, they are in America trying to reach Americans! To top it off, when they are not doing 'ministry,' they tend to spend most of their free time with other Africans. As an American under this Angolans influence, you feel used and abused. You know their hearts are pure and they want to do the Lord's work, and yet you can't help feeling angry about the situation.

How does this fictional situation make you feel? Take a moment to look again at the beginning of this chapter. Ponder your answers; perhaps you may even want to journal your thoughts. This may give you an idea of the thoughts and feelings of many of the Chinese, as we Westerners have come to China over the last 30 years. I have talked with many Chinese pastors and Christian leaders throughout the last fifteen years, and they feel like Westerners come to China to simply collect information and leave, or perhaps to get a collect a few photos with a Chinese church leader to put in a newsletter. According to them, we really don't make a very solid contribution to the Church. The Chinese have asked us to get to know them and to understand their role and purpose in ministry. Of course, I know many who have not treated the Chinese this way, but there are still many who have. In this chapter, I hope to give insight on several practical differences between Chinese and Western cultures, so that you may have a few more pieces to the Chinese puzzle.

Differences in Relationship Building

Chinese and Westerners develop relationships very differently. Traditionally in the West, we begin relationships with a certain level of trust, especially amongst people with whom we may share a common interest or life experience. In China, relationships always start with a lack of trust. Westerners are very project-oriented people; we tend to be generally friendly and open. A number of my Chinese friends have commented on this attribute. But our relationships are not very deep, and they are highly project-oriented. We enter into relationships to fulfill a mutual purpose, and once the relationship has met its purpose, we tend to drop the relationship.

The Chinese build relationships more slowly, but they tend to endure a long time. If the relationships are abused or poorly nurtured, then the Chinese can be offended. We don't understand their offense, so we often assume that they are fussy and difficult to get along with. Many Chinese have invested their entire lives developing a network of people they know and can trust. For example, if they need work done on a car, they already know someone within their network. In the relationship building process, it may take years of trust, openness, and transparency before a person may enter their network.

In business relationships, these concepts are even deeper. In the West, we follow a normal process in developing a business relationship. First, we ask ourselves if the proposed project is legal. We have a dichotomized sense about the legality of a situation. If it is illegal, we normally step out of the picture. Secondly, we ask ourselves if it is logical; we determine if we should enter into the relationship. In this part of the process, we pull out the spreadsheets, conduct the financial calculations, and explore whether or not the relationship is good for us and/or for our company. We may even create list of "pros and cons" at this stage in the process. We may ask ourselves: is this partnership valid, or are there faults or problems? Thirdly, we determine whether entering into such a project and establishing these relationships is something in which we'd like to participate. At this point, we may ask the following questions: Do I like these people? Could I see myself working well with them?

Interestingly, the Chinese process for developing business relationships is almost exactly the opposite of the Western process. They look first at whether or not the business relationship is something in which they want to be involved. If so, then they determine whether it is logical, and finally, they confront the legality of the partnership. As Westerners, we must understand how to deal with this reality. We are often concerned with ethical situations in working relationships, but in the Chinese world, one first looks at the commitment to a family member, boss, or others. As we engage with China, it is clear that they want to dialogue with us to find a common situation that may work for both sides. This will take time, patience, and diligence on our part as we understand how to build relationships from a Chinese perspective.

Legalities and Rule of Law

The onslaught of foreign companies who have set up operations in China is staggering. Since China's reopening to the West, over three decades ago, over 600,000 foreign companies have been lured to invest in China, and many of them set up offices and operations in China. I can guarantee one thing about every one of those 600,000 companies: each one had to register with the appropriate State agency that oversaw their area of industry, and each one had to pay the appropriate taxes and file the appropriate annual reports with State agencies. They also had to learn and abide by the Chinese laws dealing with their industry. By following these steps, the Government allows them to legally stay in China and continue their operations. They know this process is a reality for doing business in a foreign country.

Given this reality, I have always found it odd that only the foreign Christian community thinks it is acceptable to work outside of the laws of China. Over the last thirty years, thousands of Westerners have taken the Gospel to China. Most of these foreigners have taken a clandestine approach to ministry, due to their perceptions of their inability to openly work and live in China. By working full-time in a non-Christian job, which gives them legitimacy to legally live in China, they conduct Christian ministry during their free time.

Normally, their sending agencies instruct them to be very careful about their speech, because Chinese governmental authorities listen to their phone conversations or to conversations they have with others in public. They must watch what they say to whom, because they don't know when they will be 'found out.' In my opinion, the fear of danger and the concept of safety have caused people to take the will of God back into their own hands. I'd like to unpack this topic more fully, but I will save the unpacking for Chapter 6, as we look at constructive engagement for Westerners in modern-day China.

In the discussion of changing Western perceptions, I believe this is an important missing piece of the puzzle: when a Westerner comes to China, he has his 'Western goggles' on. He views life and discerns situations differently. The culture and environment in which each of us grew up helps us to see life from a certain perspective.

The Western concept of law implies that there is a direct relationship between the laws and how they are implemented. For example, when a person exceeds the speed limit and a policeman tracks his speed on a radar gun, a definite penalty is set by the law for that infraction. If the person is traveling twenty miles over the limit, the penalty is X; it's always going to be X—no questions asked.

In China, where relationships take precedence above everything else, people are the rule of law, not words on paper. In any given situation, the person with authority has the right to implement the law or policy of his own choosing; he can even implement a law that conflicts with the written law. Most of the Chinese assume that this liberty is a right belonging to the person in authority. And while we in the West desire to see China develop a more rigid Rule of Law, the reality is that Rule of Man is much more prevalent. The application of laws is fluid in nature. In some cases, the Chinese know that the application is more relaxed, and in other cases, the application is more restrictive. A Westerner who has arrived in China deduces one of two things:

1. Comply with Chinese laws or policies with Western rigidity; or

2. Disregard all Chinese laws, assuming they are all equally arbitrary, and assume that any individual has the right to exploit them for personal benefit.

The problem here is that the Westerner doesn't have the context within which to discern which laws are flexible and in which situations. Why do they lack the context? It's simple: they are not Chinese! The Chinese people, of course, have grown up in this environment, and they completely understand this interpretation of the law. They find it interesting that we Westerners would think of these things differently.

Given this context, it seems to me that the onus is on the Westerner to figure out this situation, upon arriving in China. The foreign worker must assume their positions properly within the confines of the written law. We are the guests and newcomers, and it is therefore our responsibility to understand and abide by the laws. Due to our lack of experience, we do not yet know the degree of flexibility in the application of these laws. This is further complicated since that the application will change from one Government department to another. As we begin our ministry, we must wisely act within the solid line of the letter of the law. Once we begin to understand the language and culture, we can begin to push out a little and test the application of the laws.

As you try to understand this concept, remember the quote from the Chinese pastor at the beginning of the chapter:

> "If there are fifteen Government regulations out there, you foreigners should follow all of them, since you are guests in this country. However, we Chinese might choose twelve of them that we follow carefully, but three of them we'll challenge, and try to get our Government to reconsider. If you foreigners challenge the Government, you force us to choose between loyalty to our Government or to a foreign group. Because of the history of foreign Christians in China, it is better if you stay here

long term, building relationships, supporting and encouraging us as friends, as we, the Chinese, lead the way for change in China."

If the outsiders are the ones challenging and disobeying the laws, it puts our new Chinese friends in a tough situation. For example, I think of the case of the 'tract bombers': foreigners who come into a Chinese city, map it out, and over the course of four or five days, and under the cover of darkness, they literally bomb the city with tracts. They put tracts in bicycle baskets, on apartment doors, around shopping malls, anywhere and everywhere they think people will see them and read them.

Traditionally, there have been two problems with the 'tract bombers.' First, although their bombing may provide some excitement and a thrilling sense of danger, it has proven to be very ineffective. Since Christianity is not a 'native' religion, and because few Chinese have had even the most simple teaching on the Bible, a 'Four Laws' type presentation in a tract makes very little sense to them. Secondly, when local officials wake up the next morning, looking for someone to blame for this outright violation of Chinese law, they usually blame the local Chinese pastors, sure that they must be the culprits in this endeavor.

To the Government official, it is only logical to blame the local Chinese Christian. So, while the foreigners have a compelling story to tell of their adventures in China to their constituents back at their home church, they've actually done more harm than good for the cause of Christ in China. In my mind, a more prudent method of evangelism would be to ask the local Chinese Christians how they may want to partner together to reach the lost in China's cities.

Imperialist vs. Immigrant Mentality

Over the years, I've kept a keen eye on the attitudes of the foreigners living and working in China. Foreigners view their time in China in two very distinct and opposing ways: they have either an Imperialist mentality or an Immigrant mentality. Between the two, there is a great distinction which shows their real attitude toward the Chinese and their calling to China.

As we saw in Chapter 1, an Imperialist mentality is one where the foreign guests in a country want to gain power and obtain indirect control over the political or economic life of that country. In the context of our attitude in modern-day China, the Imperialist mentality also includes how we treat our Chinese hosts. Do we seek to really understand their situation, especially in the Christian Church? Have we come to China as the experts on church planting, evangelism, and discipleship?

In contrast, an Immigrant comes to a country to take up permanent residence. Think about what an immigrant has to do upon arriving in a new country. Many times, he has to learn a new language, new laws, and acquire a deep understanding of how the new culture works. He must learn the new country's rules (spoken and unspoken), he has to make friends, and if he wants to make a living and support his family, he has to learn how business works in this new home. An imperialist would never think of doing all of this, because he has an attitude of superiority.

As an immigrant adjusts to a new home, he must get to know new people, often by making friends first with people on the fringes of society. People who are on the outskirts are most open to friendship, since they are outside of the mainstream. People in the center of society, the movers and shakers, aren't open to friendship with outsiders, since they already have plenty of friends within their sphere of influence. It may take years of pursuing people and developing relationships for an immigrant to be an accepted member of society, to be in a place where he can get to know the people in the center of society.

Different Leadership Styles

As we understand the culture and work in China, we must also be aware of the differences in leadership styles. In the West, a good leader deals with change; people consider him to be a change agent. Western leadership training uses terms like *vision, transformation, challenging the status quo* and *being a risk taker.* In the West, we define a good leader with terms like *passion, decisiveness, conviction,* and *self-knowledge.* In addition, individualism reigns and rules, both with the leader and throughout the organization. With an individualistic outlook, the group may be abused in deference to the individual.

In China, harmony is the foundation of Chinese culture: harmony with the people and the world around them. In the Chinese collectivist organization, the key task of a Chinese leader is to seek corporate harmony. There is a Chinese idiom that speaks of holding a bowl of water. This idiom means that the responsibilities of a leader are as fragile as holding a bowl of water. The leader must keep harmony amongst all people under his care. If a leader shows equal treatment to each person, he keeps the water in the bowl; if he shows preferential treatment to anyone, he will spill the water. A leader's role is not to serve as a change agent, but rather as a social architect, to maintain the various social fabrics.

The ramifications of this type of harmony often show themselves when the Westerner tries to share a gift with a Chinese friend. The Westerner may know that the tradition of giving gifts is quite common in Chinese society, but he will quickly learn that if you give a department supervisor a specific gift, then everyone at this supervisor's level should also receive that gift. Additionally, those who work underneath the supervisor should also receive a gift, but that gift cannot surpass the supervisors' gifts. One will quickly realize that to single out one person actually embarrasses them and damages the harmony of the office.

As we live and work in China, we also learn that structure in a Chinese company or organization is essentially authoritarian. In fact, submission to authority is interwoven so deeply into the Chinese psyche that it almost offends us Westerners. Subordinates must show respect and obedience to superiors, and those of unequal status maintain a social distance from one another to prevent familiarity, thereby destroying the order. There is pressure to preserve harmony as well as to conform, to avoid loss of face and shame. In China, the collectiveness of leaders and organizations leads to abuse of an individual out of respect and protection of the group for the good of social harmony.

As we assess the differing approaches to leadership and organizations, individualism and collectivism have become the greatest weaknesses for both systems, Western and Chinese. Westerners abuse the group for the good of the individual, and the Chinese abuse the individual for the good of the group. We must understand this information in order to be effective in our work in China.

Communication Methods

Of all the differences between the West and China, there may be none more perplexing to the Westerner that the differing styles of communication. In America, since our communities consist of people from many different backgrounds, communication comes down to one thing: speech. You better mean what you say. Since China is a homogeneous culture, communication is not only verbal, but it involves a lot of body language and other of signals. A person may say, "Oh, that's fine," while signaling his unhappiness about a situation. Here are some examples of how communication methods differ in the West and in China.

Receiving a Compliment:

In the West, when we receive a compliment about something we've done or accomplished, we quickly internalize the compliment. It makes us feel good about ourselves. In fact, we may even think to ourselves, 'I really did a good job, didn't I?' But the Chinese often deflect a compliment; they try to reverse it to compliment you or to give credit to the one who helped them achieve the accomplishment. Here is an example of a typical Chinese response:

Western Friend: "Xing, you get a great job with that project! You are so talented!"

Xing: "Oh, no, I did not do very well."

Western Friend: "Of course you did. Look at the quality of your work!"

Xing: "If it was not for you, this project would not have gone well."

Western Friend: "What do you mean? I hardly did anything. I was out of town."

Xing: "I had a good teacher who helped me learn this trade. I must continue working hard to become even better."

This dialogue can begin to drive Westerners crazy. We may think, "Just take the compliment, already!" As we develop relationships with the Chinese, we must recognize that they process much differently than we do.

Accepting an Invitation

If you've ever tried to get a Chinese friend to allow you to pay for a meal, or if you have ever invited a friend to your house for dinner, then you know how interesting this process can become. Typically, the Chinese may decline an invitation to join you for a meal. Your Chinese friend is trying to make sure that he is not projecting himself as too important. (Remember the story of the bowl of water.) In order to encourage a Chinese friend to accept your invitation, you must ask him three times before he will accept it. This shows him that you are serious about the invitation, and you are not just inviting them to be polite.

Saving Face

Westerners are often perplexed by the Chinese idea of saving face. In fact, a recent poll by the China Youth Daily showed that 87% of the Chinese public agrees that saving face is an integral part of their lives. Saving face has two aspects: saving one's own face, and saving someone else's face. A person can lose face when he appears weaker or less competent in front of someone he respect or is in competition with. Conversely, a person can gain face when others view him as good and superior in his work; this may raise his stature in their eyes.

When a Chinese friend tries to help you save face, he may try to take the humiliation onto himself, divert attention elsewhere, or propose a compromise solution that isn't so humiliating. They are trying to help you to seem more capable and competent in front of someone you may need to impress. This is a gift to you, as he tries to help you in this way.

Contrary to this idea of saving face, we Americans value direct communication; we mean what we say. We will often use phrases like, "Tell it like it is," or "Give it to me straight." But for the Chinese, 'giving it to you straight' might mean causing you to lose face, which they would never dream of doing.

This becomes frustrating when we work in business or ministry, since we feel we need to know the facts, even if it is bad news. It requires patience and understanding on both sides: our Chinese friends will learn our need for the facts, and we must allow time for them to understand that saving face is not nearly as important to us.

Expressing Feelings

In America, we are encouraged to express our feelings. In fact, if we don't develop the skill of expressing our feelings, it could have detrimental effects. The inability to express our feelings has been linked to depression, eating disorders, anger, and many additional problems. Yet in China, to refrain from overtly showing joy, sadness, or anger, the Chinese avoid imposing their feelings on others in an effort to maintain harmony. The Chinese educate their children to keep from blatantly showing feelings of anger, disappointment, or vengeance.

As you can see, we have much to learn about China and the Chinese people. China experts believe that the concerned Western Christian population needs God to develop people to become 'missionary ambassadors.' These ambassadors should understand China, learn the Chinese language, befriend Chinese government and intellectual leaders, and interpret China to the West. This would require a 10-year commitment, but it is the key task as we engage with China in the 21st Century.

Chapter 4

The Persecution Myth and Why It Survives

"Christians in America need to get over their insatiable hunger for persecution stories, and we in the house churches must get over our persecution complex. Yes, there has been persecution in this city's past, but our greatest need is not eliminating persecution but building up mature fellowship and developing unity among Christians."

—*Beijing House Church Pastor, 2006*

Myth: noun;

> 1. usually a traditional story of ostensibly historical events that serves to unfold part of the worldview of a people or explain a practice, belief, or natural phenomenon.

2. a popular belief or tradition that has grown
up around something or someone.
—*Webster's Online Dictionary*

Somehow, in our human nature and the American psyche, we are attracted to accidents and other people's pain. You know what I'm talking about: you're driving on the highway, and traffic is moving along great. Then, all of a sudden, the traffic flow comes to an immediate halt. You look down the highway to see if there is an accident, but you cannot see anything. Thirty minutes later, you drive past the scene of the 'accident,' only to find someone changing a flat tire. Yet everyone has stopped to look. In most of America, we call this phenomenon 'Rubbernecking'; in Chicago, they call this type of slowdown 'Gaper Delay.'

Whatever you call it, it is a very interesting characteristic of human nature. American researchers have found that a car with a flat tire on the side of a highway often causes as much delay as a collision, due to rubbernecking. If traffic is dense, the slowdown in traffic persists, long after the accident scene has been cleared. Traffic experts call this phenomenon a phantom accident. This behavior can cause further and potentially more serious accidents among the distracted gawkers.

Persecution of Christians in China: A Primer

In the West, when we hear stories about the persecution of Christians anywhere around the world, our hearts go out to those suffering for the sake of Christ. It is no laughing matter when one of God's children experiences persecution, because there is a human element to which we can all relate. Despite some current reports of widespread persecution of Christians in China, I believe that persecution plays a small part of the overall role in Christianity in China. My extensive research indicates continued openness of government officials towards Christianity, as indicated in earlier chapters. While there is some persecution of Christians in China, it is not widespread; it is sporadic and occasional. From this, we can conclude several indicators. There is not only the 'blessed Chinese road', on which the country and its leaders have traveled, but there is also statistical information and the firsthand accounts of Christians living in China. In order to fully discuss the situation, I'd like to present some definitions and basic information regarding the persecution situation in China.

What is persecution? The *Random House College Dictionary* defines it as 'a program or campaign to exterminate, drive away, or subjugate a people because of their religious, ethical, or moral beliefs or practices.'[1] Throughout the history of Christianity, believers in Christ have been persecuted for their faith. The Bible is clear on the subject of persecution, and God clearly brings His children through persecution as a part of His calling on our lives. Persecution is also a part of God's plan for us as Christians; it is an integral consequence of following Jesus. The Bible tells us that those who 'desire to live a godly life in Christ Jesus will be persecuted.' (1 Tim. 3:12) Believers of Christ in China have been no different throughout the last 200 years. As we've already seen, through the course of the first chapter, many Chinese Christians have suffered for their faith at the hands of the Communist Government and Chinese traditionalists.

For those who want to understand the level and severity of Christian persecution in China today, we must look through a paradigm that is more than sixty years in the making. First, let me be absolutely clear: there is no doubt that Chinese Christians suffered horribly for their faith from 1950-1970. I could write many chapters detailing the severe persecution during this dark period of Chinese history. Underneath a Communist government which viewed religion as a weakness and an 'opiate of the people,' massive persecution nearly wiped away Christianity from China. After the Communist takeover in 1949, many Chinese and Westerners fled to Taiwan, Hong Kong, Europe and the United States. Even at the point of the worst persecution, some fled to countries outside of China. Those who were first persecuted built the paradigm through which we now view Christianity in China.

The paradigm continued as the Communist government cut off all contact with the West during the 1950's and 1960's. We really didn't know what was happening in China, but we knew Communists were in charge, and we had clearly defined our opinions of Communists. In the West, we've enjoyed building a 'good guy/bad guy' view of Communism worldwide. This view, combined with a lack of familiarity with all things Chinese, has led to a tendency to cast China in a negative light.

It is a modern-day reality that while China has certainly experienced over half a century of Communistic rule, modern-day China is quickly distancing itself from its Communist past. As we look at the rapid changes that have happened in China over the last fifteen years, it's becoming harder to call China a Communist State. State-run industries are shutting down daily in China, and the private ownership of land, business, and cars are commonplace. According to *Webster's Online Dictionary*, Communism refers to a totalitarian system of government in which a single authoritarian party controls state-owned means of production.[2] If you've spent any time in China over the last few years, you know this does not define modern-day China.

Throughout the course of the 20th Century, some Western ministries have built their organization on the premise of helping the persecuted church. While these ministries tremendously heightened awareness for those suffering from persecution worldwide, they also seem to unwilling to change their view of China despite the vast changes that have taken place in the last fifteen years. While China strives to value the important role of Christians, these organizations continue to feed the Western public with old, outdated information.

In 2005, when I was first learning these concepts, I received in the mail a fundraising packet from a major American ministry; the packet contained a picture of Chinese people in 1950's clothing, with the caption, 'Your help is desperately needed to uplift persecuted Christians in China.' The picture caught my eye right away, and I noticed immediately that their clothes were terribly out of date.

Then I read the first few paragraphs:

> For nearly five decades, a billion Chinese souls have been sealed off from the Gospel. Those who have received the Good News continue to be persecuted relentlessly in the latest crackdown from the communist government. The secret police torture Christians with electric shock treatments, destroy house churches, and imprison pastors and their congregations.[3]

As I read this fundraising appeal, I determined that either this organization had been out of touch with China for a long time, or perhaps they knew of the changes in China but couldn't afford to reveal China's emerging religious freedom. Think about it: If you've built your whole ministry around persecution stories, and if your 'bread and butter' begins to fade, it would be tempting to prolong that paradigm for as long as possible. Your ministry depends on it! Calls, e-mails and first-hand meetings with organizational officials only led to more confusion, even among their own staff.

I talked to the man in charge of all promotional events and fundraising, and he was surprised that this piece had made it out of their offices at all. As I pressed him on the issues surrounding their mailer, he told me that he'd have to talk with senior management to get more information, and he promised to get back to me. I never did get a call back! I imagine that someone reminded him not to bite the hand that feeds him, and it was best to let this situation slowly fade away.

While sustaining the persecution myth is good for ministries who use those stories for fundraising purposes, it's certainly not beneficial for the rest of us, and it's definitely not good for the Church in China. The Chinese are asking us for help in certain areas of their rapid growth and development. We have the resources to help them in finances, theological training, and prayer, just to name a few. But here's what happens: when we are looking through the wrong shade of glasses, we don't see those opportunities as they really are. The death of the myth is beneficial for us; for example, when pastors know that there is a desperate need and an invitation for them to teach and train thousands of new Chinese pastors and evangelists, this deepens the ministry in China. This allows us to serve where God is already at work. We must work hard to make sure the Christian community views China through the correct set of 'glasses.'

As we'll see in the next chapter, a group of Western ministries have come together to set standards for our engagement in China. Those standards include how we receive information about China as well as how we report that information. For example, if we are paying for stories about Christianity in China, then we may not be able to trust the validity of that information. How could anyone be sure the story wasn't a good work of fiction, crafted for the sake getting the money? Further issues include telling both sides of a story, using old or outdated pictures or information, and having a verification mechanism in place. In particular, the verification issue is a really hard piece of the puzzle, and that's why most organizations don't do it. In order to verify, we must have people on the ground in China, able to speak Chinese, and familiar with the particular city or town.

Three Examples of the Need for Verification from First Edition

In March 2005, I received an email from another major Western Christian organization, whose primary goal is to aid Christians worldwide who are persecuted for their faith in Christ. The story came from Hangzhou, China, a beautiful city just west of Shanghai. Local government officials had torn down a church, and the email account of the story was verified by actual video footage of the bulldozers destroying the church. Clearly, this was yet another example of the relentless persecution of Christians in China.

Shortly after the story was published, a colleague of mine visited that same city to administer one of his organization's projects. Since he was very familiar with that city and knew many local Chinese Church officials, I asked if he would be willing to check out this story during his visit. He had also received the story, and he had planned to research the event. Upon his arrival to Hangzhou, he went to the exact location of the destroyed church. After several hours of questioning the locals in the area, he found the pastor of that church; he asked him what had happened.

The pastor took him on top of a nearby hillside to give him a better view of the area. The pastor told him that indeed his church had been torn down, along with a long row of stores attached to the church. He explained that the church was built in the late 19th century by China Inland Mission, and it desperately needed repair. The local city government planned to build a loop highway around Hangzhou, and they wanted to put the highway in the location where the church had stood for over 100 years. The local government officials offered a proposal to tear down the church and surrounding buildings for the construction of the highway; in return, they would build a new church for the congregation on the other side of the highway. The pastor showed my colleague both locations: where the old church had once stood, and where they had begun to build their new church to their specifications and needs. Indeed, a church had been torn down. But that congregation was also blessed by a new, modern, and larger facility.

Gong Shengliang has been the poster boy for persecution in China for the last several years. As pastor of the South China Church house church network, which boasts nearly 50,000 members across several provinces, he has epitomized the western view of Christianity in China. In August 2001, he was charged and convicted on charges of rape. The Jingmen Municipal People's Procurator of Hubei Province sentenced him to death. Reports spread that he regularly beat up people who refused to join the South China Church, and that he told female followers that their Christian piety was dependent on having sexual relations with him. Many were confident that the charge and sentence against him were false, and a great sentiment of sympathy went out to him. In December 2001, under international pressure led by U.S. President George W. Bush to release him, China rescinded the death penalty and sentenced him instead to life in prison. Many viewed his conviction and subsequent imprisonment as a clear case of "trumped up charges" by the Chinese government, as a way to discredit and detain Pastor Gong.

Throughout the next six years, two interesting events took place. Hundreds of thousands of Western Christians emailed and faxed appeals to the Chinese Embassies in the United States and other Western countries. At the same time, reports began to surface that certain accusations against Pastor Gong may be true, and several Western organizations began an investigation to determine the veracity of these accusations. After an extensive examination, the government determined that he was in fact guilty of the charges of rape. The evidence suggested that he seduced and molested some female members of the South China Church over a long period of time. The allegations that he used violence against those who betrayed the South China Church were also proven true. In August 2007, China Aid Association received a letter from Pastor Gong, admitting his guilt and wrongdoings that led to his arrest and imprisonment. Toward the end of his letter he wrote, "I realized that I deserve this punishment for what I have done."

I will not soon forget the morning of November 3, 2007. After my normal morning routine, I received a phone call from a friend of mine, asking if I had heard that the Bible had been put on a list of 'prohibited objects' for the athletes coming to Beijing for the 2008 Summer Olympics. Originally reported by an Italian newspaper, La Gazetta dello Sport, the English version of the story was posted on the Catholic News Agency website. The report stated that a La Gazetta reporter, attending a Beijing Olympic Organizing Committee news conference, heard an Organizing Committee member state that 'materials used for the promotion of religious or political activity' would not be allowed for the athletes at the Summer Games. Somehow, the reporter thereby inferred that the Bible would be banned. Once the story went on the Catholic News Agency website, it spread like wildfire on Catholic and Evangelical websites and blogs. The story even reached the hallowed halls of United States Congress; Senator Lindsay Graham condemned China on the floor of the Senate and encouraged President George W. Bush to boycott the 2008 Olympics and rescind his commitment to attend the Beijing Olympics. Congressman McCotter of Michigan also condemned China from the floor of the House of Representatives. The response from the Beijing Organizing Committee was clear. "The reports are nothing but blatant lies.... Bibles and religious scriptures of the major faiths brought by athletes into the Olympic village are allowed... This is the same as in all other Olympiads."[4]

As soon as I heard the Bible was on this list, I was surprised and more than a little suspicious of the story. I recalled the summer of 2005, when I visited the half-built Church in North Beijing, intended as the place of worship for athletes for the Beijing Summer Olympics. I spoke to the pastor of this church; he spoke with excitement about the opportunity to reach out and serve athletes from around the world. He told me about a project they had undertaken with the Amity Printing Press: to have Bibles printed in many languages, and to distribute them to athletes during the Summer Olympics.

After learning about the story, I decided to conduct some research for myself. I immediately emailed the United States Olympic Committee, to find out what they knew. This was their response:

> "We have received confirmation from both the International Olympic Committee and the Beijing Organizing Committee that Bibles and other religious materials will be permitted in the Athletes Village for personal use. The news reports that the Beijing Organizing Committee was considering a prohibition were completely incorrect and stemmed from a miscommunication between a journalist from Italy and a representative of the organizing committee. In addition, there will be an area in the Athletes village where athletes, coaches and officials can worship—as is always the case at the Olympic Games."

Some additional online reading revealed that the Beijing Olympic official was simply quoting from the International Olympic Charter, Rule 51, Section 3. The section, primarily intended to discourage Olympic athletes from using the Olympic stage to forward a political agenda, never mentions a prohibition of the Bible, and to infer such a prohibition is irresponsible journalism. The Catholic News Agency could have easily taken the simple steps I took to determine that the story was not true. This is especially true in a country where Christianity is growing at breakneck speed, and they are legally printing Bibles by the millions.

These three stories merely scratch the surface when it comes to the Western propagation of old paradigms about China. This is the big question: How should we respond? I think the answer is at least two-fold. First, we need to make sure that the information we read about Christianity in China comes from a reliable source. Don't be afraid to contact the source of the information, and ask them about their process of receiving and disseminating their stories on China. Secondly, we should all join a call for Western ministries to review their policies on reporting stories about China. At the very least, we should commit to these internationally recognized standards:

- Commit to only talk or write authoritatively about any aspect of Christianity in China if we have first-hand knowledge or information. (I Peter 2:1)

- Commit to seeking out the truth about Christianity in China, and only communicate what is accurate and true. Therefore, narrative about events must be current, complete and accurate. There must be no material omissions, exaggerations of fact, use of mis-leading photographs, or any other communication which could create a false impression or misunder-standing.

- If a story happened in the past, make note of it. References to past activities or events must be appropriately dated.

- If we find that a story was communicated or printed without correct facts, we must retract the story and make the correct changes.

- If anyone receives money for a story, we must note that the story was purchased.

Persecution by the Numbers

China Aid, a Midland, Texas-based organization founded by Fu Xiqiu, has become a leader in the West on reporting Chinese persecution stories. Fu, a student leader in the 1989 Tiananmen Square student democracy movement, fled to the United States through Hong Kong in 1996. According to their website, their mission is to ' expose the abuses perpetrated by the Communist Party that rules the People's Republic of China, to encourage the abused and their families by providing legal and material assistance; and to equip leaders in the free world with accurate and reliable information about the persecuted and their families as well as to present them with various avenues of action..'[5] Their reports on persecution events in China are very thorough, and they include Chinese governmental documents to support their stories. Various United States governmental agencies regularly ask Fu Xiqiu to testify about the findings in China. China Aid is most certainly the authority on persecution of Christians in China.

In March 2011, China Aid released its 2010 China Persecution Report on persecution events for the 2010 calendar year. The report, available on their website at www.chinaaid.org, reported ninety individual cases of persecution in China in 2010. With their expanding research network, it is unlikely that they would overlook many cases of persecution in China.

As I've tried to understand the veracity of persecution in China, I've developed a little mathematical exercise. To explain, I've also included the table below with my calculations.

Number of Christians in China (2010 est.)
70,000,000

Number of people in each Church (2010 est.)
100

Number of Churches in China
700,000

Number of Christian Events Annually
364,000,000

Number of Persecution Events
90

Percentage of Christian Events that saw Persecution
.000016%

Most reports of the number of Christians in China estimate an average of about 70 million Christians today. So, let's say that the average church in China has 100 people. (This is my best estimate, given the fact that some churches in China host 4,000 people on a Sunday morning, while many more consist of twenty or thirty people meeting together in an apartment or place of business.) Therefore, we can estimate that there are 700,000 churches in China today. Many of these churches are quite active, offering a Sunday morning service as well as activities on Sunday nights, Bible studies during the week, and a variety of evangelistic and outreach programs. For the sake of my mathematical exercise, I'm going to guesstimate that each of these churches would average ten separate activities in the course of any week. A little mathematical calculation indicates the potential for 364 million separate Christian activities in China during the 2010 calendar year, which is the same time period of China Aid's 2010 Persecution Report.

Through this exercise, we can visualize the number of separate Christian activities in China during 2010, but we also must realize that each one of these 364 million events carries the possibility of interruption by Chinese governmental officials, therefore qualifying as a persecution event. China Aid, an organization whose sole purpose is to expose the persecution of Christians in China, could only find ninety events out of a possible 364 million. If we convert those numbers back to the mathematical equations, we discover that .000016 percent of all Christian events in China suffered persecution. If it was one percent of all Christian activity, we probably could still surmise that persecution plays a small role in Christianity in China, because ninety-nine percent of Christian activity would still be free persecution. But this percentage is even lower! It's not one percent—it's .000002 of one percent! Think about that for just a minute... That means that it's almost as likely for a Chinese Christian to be persecuted for their faith as it is for you or I to win the lottery!

It is time for us to view China with a new paradigm. While persecution stories bring in money, if they are not wrapped with 'the belt of truth,' they only serve to further the misconceptions that pervade the Western Church. Playing off Westerners' 'car crash culture' only serves to subvert Truth: God is at work in many wonderful ways in China. As the Chinese Church grows in complexity and organization, they need us to engage in new and exciting ways. If we hold on to thirty-year-old paradigms of Christianity in China, we cannot see the new things God is doing and how He wants the Western Church to engage. In this new environment, everyone wins. God's pleased when we have a steadfast commitment to tell the truth, and those who want to engage with China need to know the real situation in China and how they can most effectively engage.

The Theology of Persecution

In God's providence, He has used persecution in the lives of Chinese Christians to build His church. With the rapid changes that have happened in China, persecution is occasional and not widespread. For those Chinese who continue to be tested by the fires of persecution, the Bible says a lot about persecution. Let's look at what God's Word says about persecution, that we may see their testing through God's eyes.

Suffering for Christ's sake
means that God loves you

Throughout the Bible, God clearly disciplines those He loves. Consider Hebrews 12:5-6, "My son, do not regard lightly the discipline of the Lord, nor be weary when reproved by him. For the Lord disciplines the one he loves, and chastises every son whom he receives." God uses persecution and suffering as a training ground for our faith, because He loves us and wants the best for us. The suffering that Chinese Christians encounter is not surprising to the Lord. He clearly saw it coming, and still He sent them to that place of persecution....because He loves them! God also uses suffering to deepen our faith and trust in Him. When you've suffered for Christ, you know how much He can carry you through, and you know what it is like to trust only in Him.

Suffering for Christ's sake
is our calling as Christians

Throughout the letters from Paul and Peter, we can see that suffering for Christ is not strange or unusual. They each tried to arm people with the truth that suffering for Christ is to be expected. This is why Peter wrote in 1 Peter 4:1, 'Since therefore Christ suffered in the flesh, arm yourselves with the same way of thinking.' Paul also tried to prepare his converts for the idea that suffering is our calling. In 1 Thessalonians 3:3-4, he wrote, 'For you yourselves know that we are destined for this. For when we were with you, we kept telling you beforehand that we were to suffer affliction, just as it has come to pass, and just as you know.'

Even Jesus said to his disciples, "If the world hates you, know that it has hated me before it hated you. If you were of the world, the world would love you as its own; but because you are not of the world, but I chose you out of the world, therefore the world hates you. Remember the word that I said to you: 'A servant is not greater than his master.' If they persecuted me, they will also persecute you. If they kept my word, they will also keep yours." (John 15:18-20, ESV)

Some reporters cultivate the image that the persecution of Christians in China is the worst thing in the world, as though we need to do everything we can to stop it from happening. Any amount of persecution taking place in China is not terrible, nor should we stop it. As I have illustrated, these Christians experience persecution because they are in the middle of God's will for their lives, and He wants to get the glory in the midst of their persecution. We need to pray that God would use their persecution to advance His Kingdom, and that they may serve as an example of what happens to Christians who are completely sold out to the cause of Christ.

Persecution is the Occasion of Divine Triumph

As we've seen throughout the course of Chinese history, nothing can stop the growth of the Word of God. Man and governments may erect obstacles against it, but God's purpose cannot be overcome. In fact, persecution does not stop the growth of the Word, but rather it functions as its catalyst, ironically.

The proclamation of the Word spreads because of persecution. In talking to Chinese Christians who have suffered through intense persecution, they rejoice at the opportunity to suffer for the Lord's sake. They stand in agreement with Romans 5:3, "….we rejoice in our sufferings, knowing that suffering produces endurance, and endurance produces character, and character produces hope…" They'll tell you that prison was their seminary, and the experience has molded their theology and helped them to understand God's provision at a deeper level.

Suffering for Christ's Sake
Reminds Us of our Real Home

The suffering that happens to Christians for Christ's sake is a wonderful, tangible reminder of where are real home, our treasure, and our citizenship lie. Persecution is but a temporary situation, but our future with Christ spans into eternity. Paul illustrates this principle beautifully in Philippians 3:20, "But our citizenship is in heaven, and from it we await a Savior, the Lord Jesus Christ."

Even as Christians in China experience persecution, they know that nothing they've experienced in their lives on earth will compare with the treasure that awaits them in Heaven.

[1] *Random House College Dictionary*. p. 234

[2] *Merriam-Webster's Dictionary*. "Communism-Definition." [Online] March 21, 2008. < http://www.merriam-webster.com/dictionary/communism>

[3] Open Doors Fund Raising Insert, October 2006

[4] Shanghai Scrap Blog, reporting on a South China Morning Post article. [Online] November 8, 2007. http://shanghaiscrap.com/?p=373.

[5] China Aid. "Mission: China Aid." [Online] March 1, 2008. <http://chinaaid.org/about/mission/>.

Chapter 5

Beijing's Unregistered Churches

"Si fueris Romae, Romano vivito more; si fueris alibi, vivito sicut ibi (if you are in Rome, live in the Roman way; if you are elsewhere, live as they do there)."

—*Aurelius Ambrosius, better known as Saint Ambrose (4th Century A.D.)*

As you've just read in the previous chapter, it is my contention that persecution plays a small role in the overall picture of Christianity in China. Every measurable statistic, together with a considerable number of interviews and experiences in China, tells us that this is true. Since the first publication of this book in 2008, a unique situation has developed in the Chinese capital of Beijing: their unregistered churches have been able to grow largely unfettered. While most of these churches continue to minister without restriction, several are

97

pushing the boundaries of what is allowable in China and are demanding more rights as they grow in size. Given the Western media attention these churches have been getting, I hope to give you a realistic picture of the unregistered church situation in Beijing, both as a clarifying point to help you understand what's happening there, and to help you understand the situation regarding unregistered churches in China.

Laws and Policies Concerning Religious Freedom and the Right to Assemble

As I mention in several places in this book, in China there is often a difference between the written laws and the enforcement of those laws. In order to understand these unregistered churches and the environment in which they exist, I will list the rules and laws that pertain to unregistered church activity, then I'll describe how these laws are actually implemented.

The State Administration for Religious Affairs (SARA) functions under China's State Council. SARA oversees the operation of China's five officially sanctioned religious organizations: Buddhism, Taoism, Islam, Catholicism, and Protestant Christianity. SARA's administrative organization subdivides its responsibilities; from the national level, each province has its own SARA office to supervise religious activity. Each sanctioned religion has an association which oversees that religious body. In the case of Protestant Christianity, the Three-Self Patriotic Movement (TSPM) supervises all Christian activity and represents the state-recognized organization for Christianity.

SARA requires religious organizations and sites for religious activities to register with their offices. Applications must comply with the following basic requirements: a permanent location and official name, regular attendance by a core membership, a management organization composed of religious adherents, qualified clerical personnel for officiating religious activities, published management regulations, and lawful income. Christian churches seeking registration must meet each of these requirements.

In 2005, the national office of SARA issued their Regulations on Religious Affairs,[1] which were then promulgated by the State Council on March 1st. These regulations apply to all religious activity in China and encompass citizens' rights of religious belief. They also determine religious organizations' rights to publish materials that pertain to their faith (it is this provision that allows Amity to print so many Bibles), the establishment of institutes for religious education, and the specific rights of religious personnel to conduct religious activities. Fifteen articles pertain specifically to the discussion in this chapter; Chapter III, Articles 12-26 describe the site regulations for religious activities.

In order to acquire a site for religious activity in China, applicants must go through a series of steps. First, they apply for registration with the county level SARA office for official recognition. The office must respond to the application within 30 days. This application must show a need for the religious site, name trained religious personnel to oversee the location and its activities, assure the existence of the necessary funding to conduct activities, and prove the site is located in an area that won't interfere with the normal daily life of its neighbors. As a side note, this process actually works well in rural areas of China. With the church building that China Resource Center is involved in, we see this application process give rural Christians a legal way to build a church, worship, and fellowship in a safe and lawful manner.

In addition to the Chapter III articles, there exists another government communication pertinent to Beijing's unregistered churches. According to a white paper published by the Information Office of the State Council entitled "Freedom of Religious Belief in China," "There is no registration requirement for..."house services," which are mainly attended by relatives and friends for religious activities such as praying and Bible reading."[2]

This second communication raises some ambiguity for churches. On one hand, they are expected to register and meet the qualifications outlined in the Chapter III Articles cited above. On the other hand, the widespread under-standing is that registration is not required for activities that only entail praying and Bible reading. The white paper clearly sanctions activities which are smaller in size, located within a believer's home and that are seen as a regular part of a Christian's life. It is this perception under which most of China's unregistered church groups operate; most assume that they are allowed to assemble without registering and enjoy a bit of autonomy. According to this white paper, there exists a legal precedent for believers to meet in an apartment. Consequently, Beijing's unregistered churches meet quite openly, freely and without restriction. In contrast, while most pastors in registered churches in Beijing are able to preach without restriction, they understand that the approval process for registered sites moves at a very slow pace. Many unregis-tered church leaders don't have the patience to register or the fortitude to wait, given how openly they operate without such endorsements today.

While Beijing's officials seem more than willing to allow the unregistered churches to hold Sunday services and conduct church activities during the week, there exist several unspoken rules. For example, an unregistered church in Beijing should not become overtly political by asking for more legal recognition, nor should it involve foreign groups that might cause the government to lose face. The majority of Beijing officials give the strong impression that they are happy to operate within a gray area by their willingness to 'look the other way' when it comes to unregistered church groups. We in the West always want situations defined in black and white terms. In China, however, most citizens are happy to live in the gray areas between black and white. It seems odd to

Westerners for China to have regulations about sites for religious activity, but not to enforce them. While these contradictions show apparent imprudence in the Chinese legal system, it is not for us to change their way of thinking but rather to adapt to their willingness to operate within gray areas. Flexible thinking on our part will allow us to participate more fully in their religious life and practices.

Beijing's Unregistered Churches: Common Threads

It is within the gray area that most unregistered churches in Beijing thrive. My 2011 investigation revealed that a vast majority of them operate without any interference from officials. Furthermore, I identified several commonalities shared by these churches. First, the vast majority of them have taken the initiative to establish active relationships with their local police offices. In Chinese cities, the police, better known as the Public Security Bureau (PSB) maintain local sub-stations in each neighborhood. These PSB offices are operated by officials who live in the neighborhoods where they work, so they become well acquainted with the 'goings on' around their sub-stations. When my family first moved to China, we reported to the PSB office in Tianjin, since every foreigner must check in with the local officials upon arrival. A Beijing friend told me that while the "Shouwang incident" was happening in 2010, local PSB offices invited the unregistered church leaders in their areas for tea to remind them not to cause any trouble. The church leaders' response: "We don't plan to cause any trouble!"

Secondly, a vast majority of the unregistered churches in Beijing told me they were quite happy with the governmental status quo. While many of them would like to see a clear, streamlined process for legal recognition in the future, they were quite happy with the environment in which they currently worked. One of these leaders told me that he did not know of another church outside of Shouwang that was in any trouble with local authorities; given the Western perception about China's unregistered churches, this statement was surprising to me.

Finally, I found that most unregistered church leaders in Beijing know that they must keep their congregations small. This is a key for their continued prosperity. When a congregation begins to get big, over 300, it becomes more noticeable. Once churches reach a certain size, it is quite normal for them to split off and start another unregistered church. Most unregistered churches in Beijing have standard protocol that they use to train new leadership and equip new congregations with the resources they need to succeed. As an American friend who lives in China quipped, "The Beijing Government is actually aiding the effort of spreading the Gospel [there]. By encouraging the splitting off of churches, it ensures there is a Christian presence in more areas of Beijing!" He is correct; each of the unregistered churches serves as a hub for the Gospel in the neighborhoods where they exist and more people know where they can go to learn about the Christian faith.

I will introduce you to two of Beijing's unregistered congregations, Shouwang Church and Beijing Zion Church, both of which have received a fair amount of Western publicity for their differing approaches to governmental interactions. In particular, Shouwang Church's experience is not common in Beijing.

Pushing the Boundaries: Shouwang Church

Of the 3,000 or so unregistered churches in Beijing, Shouwang Church has received most of the Western publicity. Its name means "keeping watch," and at its peak, the church boasted 1,000 members. It was founded by Jin Tianming in 1993; three years earlier he had become a Christian while studying chemical engineering at Beijing's Tsinghua University. Jin and his wife started a Bible study in their home and a year later they rented an apartment to accommodate their growing fellowship. By Christmas 1997, they had organized several Christmas basket and caroling events in Beijing's neighborhoods and saw hundreds converted to Christ. By 2002, 13 fellowships had split from the original church body. The church continued to see an increase in membership, primarily made up of young professionals. In 2008, the leadership decided to consolidate their smaller, house based worship services into one bigger congregation. Once they consolidated, they began raising money for a permanent location. They eventually raised over $4 million (US) and in late 2009, purchased the second floor of the Daheng Science and Technology Tower in Northwest Beijing.

After Shouwang Church had paid for the property, the building owner began to receive pressure from local authorities; he then refused to hand over the keys to the church's second floor real estate. Shouwang leaders organized Sunday services in a local park nearby since they didn't have a place to meet. This action enflamed local officials since Chinese citizens don't have the right to public assembly. After a few weeks, local officials finally provided a location for the congregation to meet in a nearby restaurant. This situation didn't last long however, and Shouwang Church began meeting outside again. It was in April 2011 that the situation for Shouwang began to get really unpleasant.

Local PSB officials began to remove people who were attending the outdoor service, citing their lack of rights to publicly assemble. A month later, the pastors and elders at Shouwang Church wrote a petition to the State Council entitled, "We Stand Up for Our Faith—A Petition to the National People's Congress Concerning the Conflict between Church and State."[3] The petition, also signed by fifteen other unregistered church leaders in Beijing, Xi'an, Chengdu and Shanghai, pressed the State Council to re-write the religious laws in China and to adopt new laws to protect religious faith. Pastor Jin was placed under house arrest and the church effectively disbanded. Many in the congregation disagreed with the leadership's public push against the Beijing government. A former elder of the church started his own unregistered church with several former Shouwang members.

Shouwang Church pressed many issues that most of Beijing's unregistered churches had purposely avoided: they took a strong political stance with their petition, they grew far too large to avoid notice and attention and they demanded rights from the local government. It's no wonder they ran into so much trouble!

A More Balanced Approach: Beijing Zion Church

In researching unregistered churches in Beijing, I thought it would be interesting to attend one. I had recently read a *Wall Street Journal* article about the Beijing Zion Church, led by Pastor Jin (Ezra) Mingri.[4] The article outlined Pastor Jin's role among pastors who were testing government policy as it related to Beijing's unregistered churches.

Since I had a friend in common with the senior pastor of Beijing Zion Church, I was quite interested in attending a Sunday service. I hoped I would be welcomed if I showed up unannounced. With that purpose in mind, I ventured away from my Beijing hotel one Sunday morning in December of 2011 to see what I could find out. I found the church's website, complete with location, service times and archived sermons.[5] Since it wasn't far from my hotel, it didn't take me long to travel there. Approaching the location, it was not immediately apparent that a church met anywhere nearby. I walked around the neighborhood and found the building where the church met; from the outside it appeared to be a local karaoke bar. Having never attended an unregistered church before, I felt somewhat nervous about what to expect and I certainly didn't want to get any of the regular attenders in trouble by my presence. I had heard stories about American friends who had had to be shuttled to unregistered church services under cover of darkness for fear that their participation would arouse suspicion.

Once I arrived, I paced outside the building for a bit just to get a feel for what was happening and to see if there was any police monitoring in place. It all seemed surprisingly normal: cars pulled up, wives and kids would get out; chatty young people with instruments casually strolled in; two women disappeared into the dark entrance while checking their smart phones. After 10 minutes or so, seeing there clearly were no police around and that no one acted concerned about who was coming and going from the building, I asked a young man if I could enter with him. I told him, in Chinese, that I was interested in attending the service, but didn't want to cause any trouble as a foreigner.

Clearly a young professional, he replied in perfect English, "Sure, we get foreign friends joining us all the time! Why don't you come in with me?" I felt comforted by his words as he and I walked in together. Several other people joined us on the elevator ride to the 5th floor. "Where are you from?" he asked. After I told him I was visiting from Colorado, he replied, "I went to the University of Florida for my graduate work." Comforted by his familiarity with America, he and I chatted away about his experience in Florida until we reached our floor.

As the elevator doors opened, I was a little taken aback by all the activity. Kids were running around, two ladies stood behind tables selling Christian books and other materials, a woman was signing people up for a volunteer project to deliver Christmas baskets to local senior citizens. I was immediately welcomed by another lady who was handing out bulletins for the morning's service. I asked her as well if my participation would be problematic and she warmly invited me to join them. Since I hadn't been able to contact the pastor in advance and I really wanted to interview him, I also asked her how I might be able to contact him. "Hold on just a minute.... I'll get him for you." About three minutes later, Pastor Jin emerged from the sanctuary and welcomed me to his church. I told him how excited I was to be with them and how I'd love to visit with him afterward. He heartily agreed and told me that he would spend some time with me after the service.

Walking into the sanctuary, I noticed two things right away: first, it was a full room, with about 300 people busily chatting away. It was hard for me to find a seat and I learned that this was just one of three Sunday morning services. I also noticed how much it looked like a Western church, with flat screen televisions placed throughout the room, a cross attached to the wall behind the pulpit and more modern musical instruments than most registered churches would use. The four ladies serving as worship leaders were preparing for their duties at the front of the sanctuary.

The service itself was wonderful. I enjoyed great singing, watching people actively involved in worship; I listened to a great sermon from Pastor Jin from Romans 8, with timely illustrations and witty comments. During the service, a number of congregants raised their hands in praise to God. I thoroughly enjoyed the entire worship experience. Afterward, I waited about 15 minutes for Pastor Jin to finish his duties so he and I could spend some time together.

An Interview with Pastor Jin

We were able to find a room toward the back of their 5th floor facility to spend some time talking together. Pastor Jin lived up to every compliment I had heard about him; he was very warm and open, welcoming of new friends, and clearly concerned for his congregation and for lost people. Our time together shed some light on several subjects that I wanted to know more about. Here are some excerpts from my interview with him:

> MFF: I'm interested to know your overall impressions of Beijing's unregistered church situation.

> JMR: Unregistered churches in Beijing continue to get bigger and bigger. Once your church gets to a certain size, you begin to attract more attention. This is a challenge for most pastors. Once your church gets to more than 50 people, you either need to split off and start other churches or take the risk and find a location where you can meet the needs of your growing congregation. This is where good relationships are key, both with your local PSB office and your landlord. If your relationships are good and you spend time with those people, you can find a way to grow your church and reach more with the Gospel.

> MFF: I've heard that you previously were a registered church pastor. What caused you to become an unregistered church pastor?

> JMR: Yes, I was a pastor at Beijing's Gongwangshi Church. I quit that position to pursue further theological training at Fuller Seminary in California. When I finished my doctorate, I came back to Beijing to continue ministry. My former boss took me out to dinner and said, "You can lead either Gongwangshi or Chongwenmen, both registered churches in Beijing...you choose." I didn't like the tone he took, especially since it wasn't something for me to decide. I wanted to be able to pray about the decision, but he needed an answer right then. I decided to start Beijing Zion instead and today we have about 1,000 people at our church.

MFF: Given what has happened with the Shouwang Church over the last couple of years, what is your perspective on their approach in Beijing?

JMR: In Beijing today, there is a model that works for larger unregistered churches. I mentioned earlier about relationships and that helps a church like ours. Shouwang has been a trailblazer in the area of pushing the local government for more rights. There is a Chinese saying that applies here: 'The first bird that flies out of the tree gets shot.' A lot of unregistered pastors think that Shouwang is being too aggressive and are going too far, especially given the ways that a church can operate pretty well by keeping a low profile. I think that if Shouwang hadn't pushed the envelope, other churches, maybe even ours, may be getting more attention from Beijing officials. We're also pushing the envelope with our size and the scope of our ministry. A lot of ministry tools I learned while at Fuller we're using here in Beijing.

MFF: What is the biggest challenge you face in your ministry in Beijing?

JMR: By far, the biggest challenge we face is that while we work and operate quite openly and freely, we are not technically a legal entity. This is the problem that Shouwang had with the office building situation. Since they had no legal recognition, the government used that reasoning to not allow them to purchase the property that they had paid for. This is our biggest challenge as well. It makes it hard for us to purchase property and hire staff.

MFF: What is your prediction of the future of the relationship between the Beijing government and Beijing's unregistered churches?

JMR: For now, both sides are trying really hard to prove their point, but no one really prevails. I could see a stalemate of sorts, since the status quo is working relatively well. We continue to pray however, for a loosening of the government's regulations to allow us to achieve some type of legal standing in China.

MFF: I have heard from registered and unregistered church pastors that the registered church system (TSPM) is losing its influence in China today. Having been a pastor in both systems, would you agree?

JMR: I think the fact that there are only 15 registered churches in Beijing versus 3,000 unregistered churches tells you something. The organization over the registered church has been too slow to adapt to the growing interest and conversion rate that Christianity has seen, both in Beijing and all over China.

Conclusions

I have three concluding thoughts as I summarize Beijing's unregistered church situation. First, the conditions in Beijing are clearly not as bad as some would want you to think. As I've mentioned before, 'doom and gloom' is what raises funds, and portraying a Beijing government that is out to ban churches plays well with donors. The fact that I found only one unregistered church in real trouble with the Beijing officials speaks volumes about the overall state of affairs. The organizations that reported on the Shouwang church want readers to believe that their situation is mirrored all over

Beijing and China; this is simply not true. Case in point: remember The *Wall Street Journal* article I mentioned earlier in this chapter about Beijing Zion Church? The title of the article was "China's Banned Churches Defy Regime." The use of the word *banned* in the title is notable, mainly because unregistered churches in Beijing are not actually banned. Over 3,000 of them operate without government interference. If churches were banned, they would be shut down and prohibited from existing.

Secondly, we in the West can be thankful that Beijing's unregistered churches operate with relative freedom. As one Western observer told me recently, "This situation would be unheard of just ten years ago. What's happening in Beijing today is truly remarkable." The fact that all but one of Beijing's unregistered churches have no problems with local officials attests to the overall freedom in which they operate. My Beijing Zion experience is proof positive that Beijing's unregistered churches have a model that will allow them to flourish there.

Given this reality, my third conclusion is that China's Regulations on Religious Affairs are woefully out of date and are in need of a massive overhaul to reflect current realities. Creating some type of legal recognition for churches is crucial; done properly, such recognition would be a benefit to both the unregistered churches and to the Beijing government. Years ago, the Beijing government 'let the cat out of the bag' by giving the impression that registration is not required for activities that entail praying and Bible reading. After that type of perceived freedom, it's really hard to put the 'cat' back in the bag. In my misguided teenage years, I once put a cat in a microwave oven (I didn't turn it on). I can attest to the fact that putting a cat in a bag, a microwave, or anywhere it does not want to go is very hard. It's the same for these officials. They deeply underestimated what happens when Christians grow in spiritual understanding—their foundations grow deeper, which in turn leads to an interest in expanding ministry opportunities. Christians certainly want to lead non-Christians to faith in Christ. In turn, this expansion leads to larger churches that are growing in depth of mission, vision and strategic values. A new process that allows these churches to attain legal status within China makes sense for all involved. Churches would get the legal recognition they desire and the government would have a way to set regulations and monitor church activity.

Until the day such changes might be set in place, I think we can modify the popular phrase about how to behave in Rome: 'when in Beijing, do as the Beijingers do,' or perhaps better put, 'when in Beijing, do as much as the Beijing government will allow you to do.' The gray area that exists within the Beijing government's Administration of Religious Affairs Regulations gives churches a certain amount of freedom in which to operate. Most of Beijing's unregistered church pastors are happy to have the breathing room that once they did not have. For them, current policy represents a change for the better. While they would appreciate more room to operate, they don't feel a need to push very hard. The current model works quite well: have tea with the local PSB officer on a regular basis and when the church gets too big split off and add another church to the network. And in the case of Beijing Zion, they haven't even felt the need to split. They believe that if they are good neighbors, contributing to the social well-being of the area, authorities will see them as a beneficial presence. Given their attitude, I believe our response should be to pray for increased latitude and legal recognition for all churches in China.

---

[1] http://chinesejil.oxfordjournals.org/content/5/2/475.full
[2] http://www.china.org.cn/e-white/Freedom/f-3.htm
[3] http://www.cabsa.org/article_detail.php?type=18&aid=273
[4] http://blogs.wsj.com/chinarealtime/2011/07/28/reporters-notebook-inside-chinas-underground-churches/
[5] http://www.zionchurch.cn

Chapter 6

New Opportunities for Westerners in China

"Chinese Christians will tell you without exception that they are gaining freedom. We are just on the verge of something happening when Christianity is going to be completely tolerated. We say to government groups, "Will you allow us to let the Chinese church into areas of orphanages, arts, education? Without hesitation, they reply, 'Yes, but you have to get permission for it first.'"[1]

— *Robert Cheely, from Jesus in Beijing*

My Involvement in China: A Case Study

My involvement in China has spanned a very crucial period in China's history. Since my first trip to China in 1996, I have witnessed many significant changes in the country, including the transformation into a market economy. I have seen firsthand the beginning of the massive restructuring of that nation. Since my experience in China started after the tumultuous 1980's, I've always viewed China from a different perspective than many of my fellow Western laborers, especially those who first came into China after the reopening to the West in the 1980's. I have been able to accomplish the mission for my ministry through opportunities to work successfully with registered church and government officials.

Through my journey of involvement in China, three things have happened. First, I've embraced and functioned beneath ministry models set in place by organizations that entered China after the reopening. Because they returned to China while they felt their safety and security were at risk, they developed a set of guidelines for their China service. Secondly, I've seen firsthand how government officials, at all levels in China, have greatly appreciated and responded to my openness to developing relationships. Throughout my ministry, my objective has always been to portray Western Christians as people of good will. Thirdly, I have met others who have taken this same approach, and I have developed deep partnerships with others who have worked more openly. I have learned a great deal from them, and I am thankful for their contributions to my mode of operation in China.

As foreign organizations came into China during the 1980's, they knew two things. They knew that the Chinese government had tried for thirty years to eliminate Christianity. Reports of massive persecution continued to filter out of China, through the testimonies of Chinese who escaped and the occasional foreigner who snuck into the country. They also knew the Chinese government didn't like foreigners very much. Even after ending its period of self-isolation, China allowed foreigners to visit only its major cities through most of the 1980's.

In his book, *Jesus Never Left China*[2], Dr. Werner Burklin gives a gripping account of his re-entry into China in the early 1980's. At every turn, the Chinese officials told him, "You can't be here. What are you doing?" Within this context, many foreign organizations set up their mode of operation as they reentered China. With safety and security as the overarching goals, this mode was characterized by the use of code language while in public, since they did not know who may have been listening to their conversations, and they did not want to reveal that they were Christians. As an example, they used the word 'book' instead of 'Bible,' or they said 'building' when they meant 'church.' They assumed that the government had placed 'monitors' throughout their city, listening in to foreigners' conversations. They worked fulltime in non-Christian jobs, such as teaching English or starting a small company, which gave them legitimacy under the law to live in China. Most foreigners felt they had to 'subvert' their true intentions in China with a clandestine ministry in the country.

During the first two decades after China's reopening to the West, God clearly blessed and used this approach. Those foreigners have been an especially effective Christian presence, teaching English at China's universities. Teaching English has given them contact points with many Chinese, some of whom already know some English. The open secret has been that these are not just regular English teachers; they are also committed and serious Christians who are vocal about their faith. During the last three decades, the Chinese government, while occasionally irked by how vocal these Christians can be about their faith, has also come to appreciate the quality of their work and their exemplary behavior. They don't get in trouble, they show up for their classes, they are well prepared, and they don't flirt with local Chinese girls. I have met many young Chinese Christians, both in China and on U.S. Campuses, who have come to faith in Christ through the influence of a Western English teacher.

When I entered the China scene in the mid-1990's, this well-established paradigm was the expectation for anyone working with major organizations in China. Since I wasn't involved in China during the 1980's, perhaps I came with a fresh perspective and open eyes to see China with different lenses. It was my privilege to meet local government officials, and I found them to be just like government officials everywhere. These men and women wanted to impress their bosses; they wanted to do just enough work to keep their jobs, and if someone could help them accomplish that, then they welcomed a partnership opportunity. As my experiences began to deepen and unfold, I started to wonder about the Western organizations' mode of operation in China. Were the secrecy and security measures necessary? After a number of years of traveling to China, talking with both Western and Chinese friends and assessing current realities, I determined of my own volition that working with openness and transparency allowed for greater untapped opportunities than the 'secrecy and security' method, propagated by many Western organizations. Throughout many meetings with officials, I found that they were pleased that I had taken the time to meet them to listen to their concerns and hopes.

My choice to live in China and conduct language study at the start of the 21st century gave me an opportunity to test some of my theories about the changing nature of working and living in China. My findings were nothing short of miraculous, given the paradigm I had for working in China. The 'secrecy and security' methods of the 1980's had created a clouded bubble that caused foreigners to miss the emerging possibilities in 21st Century China. I had several meetings and conversations with Western friends, and their perspectives confirmed my theory. For example, in 2001, I met with a friend who had been in China since 1987. I asked him, "What is the real threat that we face from the Chinese government? Do you really think the government will persecute you, simply because you are a Christian?" His response was the clincher. He said, "No, Mike, I don't believe that. But we've been working under this paradigm for so long now that it would be hard for us to make a change."

In that moment, I committed in my heart and mind to find a better way to be involved as an American in China. I searched for others who had possibly made the same discoveries, and I found the 'faithful few' who had also determined to work in an open manner. Often criticized in the West for 'sleeping with the enemy,' they had burst the clouded bubble of the old regime. My favorite story, albeit sad, tells of a friend who attended a China Ministry conference in the U.S. At lunchtime, he chose a table filled with people he wanted to meet. After he sat down at the table, several people got up and left; they told him that they couldn't eat with him since he worked with the registered church. How sad that two groups can be so diversified, when our mission is ultimately united.

Working with Transparency in China

For many of the Westerners who are concerned about China, the idea of engaging with Chinese governmental officials makes as much sense as shooting oneself through the head. Since the Chinese Communist Party has tried so rigidly to control religion in the past, they rationalize that they must stay far away from governmental officials when they are trying to reach Chinese for Christ. However, China has undertaken the most dramatic change of any country in the history of the world. It is almost unbelievable to think about the change that has taken place from 1977 to 2012. These changes have brought a dramatic shift in the Chinese governments' attitude toward Christians and Christianity. Numerous speeches by high-ranking Chinese officials throughout the last few years have revealed that the Chinese government views Christians as a benefit and a great social stabilizer to Chinese society. As a result, when Western Christian organizations are willing to work with a new degree of openness and transparency, they find new opportunities.

As we have discussed, relationships are very important to the Chinese people. We must practice great patience over many years to develop deep and trusting relationships in China, with both Chinese citizens and government officials. The people in government circles understand that most Westerners are Christians, and they are watching us. As we choose to come as learners, with a humble attitude toward government officials, our actions will reflect negatively or positively on Christianity. Everyone likes to be treated with respect, to be looked in the eye, to be greeted with a warm handshake; Chinese governmental officials are no different. The ethic of reciprocity, or the Golden Rule (to treat others as you would want to be treated), makes sense in a place like China. Each person must earn credibility, and relationships are a driving force in the society. Xing Zihui, a teacher in an unregistered seminary, agrees. In a *Wall Street Journal* article in 2005, he states, "You have to realize that China's not a strict place. If your relations with officials are good, you can do whatever you like, as long as there's no trouble."[3]

Most China watchers agree: there is no longer a need to hide our identity as foreign Christians. People have begun to recognize that credibility must be earned; as they live and love like Jesus, they can be vessels of change in the decisions of the Chinese government. As the old saying goes, 'There's no impact without contact.' In addition, this style of engagement recognizes the Biblical principal of God-given authority, found in Romans 13. This passage says that God has ordained, instituted, and given authority to governments, so to resist their authority is to resist God. Matthew Henry, the 16th Century Bible commentator wrote about this passage, "However the persons (of the government) themselves may be wicked... yet the just power which they have must be submitted to and obeyed."[4] This is yet another reflection of the credibility of Christ. Chinese government officials are wary of those activities that continue to be clandestine in nature, and this wariness is not unique to China: The United States government, which created the Department of Homeland Security after the September 11th attacks on American soil, also passed the USA Patriot Act for the sole purpose of knowing what is happening in secret. Regarding Westerners in China, the only thing these officials fear is that which they don't know about.

This monumental shift in ministry perspective has also spread to those formerly trained to maintain the 'secrecy and security' method. An American friend of mine, trained by his sending agency to watch carefully his words and emails, recently shared this story with me. As the local representative for the International Fellowship in his city (population 10 million) in China, he must attend a monthly meeting for the Religious Affairs Bureau (RAB). "As the representative for our fellowship, I have to go to a city-level meeting once a month. I don't do much at the meeting, except to give a two-minute report on our Fellowship. But I give my report at the end, so I have to sit through the whole two-hour meeting.

The leader of our city's RAB started the meeting by announcing that he had just gotten word from the National government saying they need to do more to make life easier for their city's Protestant Christians. So, the following two hours were a brainstorming session for the city's Government leaders, listing ways they can encourage the Christians in their city. In hearing this news and the subsequent discussion, I was so impressed with the level of dialogue; when the time arrived for me to give my presentation, I asked for additional time to address the whole crowd. I told them I was deeply encouraged by the level of dialogue, and I pledged to help them achieve their goals in any way possible. They asked if I could be on a task force to help in this process, and I was compelled to help and serve them in this way."

Since the publication of the 1st edition of this book, there are many more organizations who are now seeing opportunities to work more openly in China. In fact, one of the largest Christian organizations in the United States also has a major presence in China. They have moved their China HQ from Singapore to Beijing or Shanghai and have regular meetings with appropriate Government officials.

Ethical Foundations for China Service

As I watched firsthand how others served in China, we created a bond and embraced an opportunity to share what we had learned in working openly in China. After several informal meetings with a group of 6-8 people, we decided to gather as many China ministry leaders as we could to create guidelines for this open approach to service. A select group of leaders wholeheartedly agreed with the need, and they proposed that we begin talking about these 'standards,' their purpose, and for whom they would be written. After several meetings in the U.S. and China over the course of two years, we finished our *Ethical Foundations for China Service*. We concluded our discussion and wrote the Foundations at a Symposium sponsored by my organization at Fuller Seminary in June 2006. In developing these Foundations, we hoped to offer guidelines for the most effective service in China.

It is not unusual to undertake the practice of creating an 'industry' standard. In the corporate world, standards of business practices or operational standards are commonplace. Even within our Christian circles, many Christians have come together to guide the believing community to a higher standard. The Evangelical Council for Financial Accountability is a good example of this type of internal accountability. Numerous Christian areas of service also operate within a standard of conduct, as well as many Christian colleges and universities. The Apostle Paul portrayed this attitude as well. In 2 Corinthians 8:21, he writes, 'For we aim at what is honorable, not only in the Lord's sight but also in the sight of man.'

Upon completion, we offered these guidelines to sup-port the China-concerned community and to encourage Westerners to think of ways to optimize our service in China. We hoped that each organization involved in China would embrace these Foundations as a starting point to pursue the most effective service in China. The Foundations in their entirety are found in Appendix A of this book. In this chapter, allow me to offer the main points of each Foundation, together with some commentary on each one.

> Recognizing the changes in China, the signifi-cant growth in the Church in China, and the complexity of Chinese society and its regulatory structures, we offer these guidelines for service in China and to support the Christian commu-nity in China.

We will demonstrate the credibility and relevance of Jesus Christ through our words and actions. We believe that government circles understand that most Westerners are Christians. This implies that our actions will reflect Christianity, either negatively or positively. Of those who watch and study China, most people agree that there is no longer a need to hide our Christian identity. We believe that in our attempt to be relevant, we must evaluate if are we posi-tioning our message about Christ in reference to what the Chinese people are asking for. Many people agree that in everything we do in China, we must always acknowledge Christ; we must not allow 'security concerns' to override our desire to bring Christ to the Chinese people.

We will strive to respect local government, regula-tions, culture, history, and aspirations of the Chinese people. As I mentioned previously, my organization is not alone in finding success by respecting local government. Increasingly, more and more organizations and individuals find that they can fulfill their mission while taking the time to earn the trust of Chinese officials. Therefore, we must have an 'immigrant' mentality, knowing that we come to China as guests, not as 'colonialists.' Far too often, we Westerners think we know the best way for the Chinese to impact their country, even before we've invested time in relationships to determine how the Chinese system works. We need to be careful to learn the agenda of local Chinese agencies before we present our own. The people we talked with accepted these ideas easily, and many people expressed a desire to learn how to better understand and implement these standards.

We will serve the whole body of Christ in China and promote its harmony and self-sufficiency. This area of service in China is multifaceted. In choosing the word 'serve,' we wanted to support and encourage the Chinese Christians to take the lead in the Christian community. We also wanted to emphasize the need to recognize the many facets of the Church in China. We tend to think divisively, focusing on the differences between a rural church, an urban church, an open church, a house church, a professional church, and a working class church. Instead, Westerners need to view the Church in China as a whole.

To continue, we believe it is important to communicate to the Chinese and others the truth that God wants us to be part of the reconciliation in the body of Christ in China. There is the issue of self-sufficiency in the Chinese Church, and we must make sure that we do not allow outside funds to set the agenda for Christians in China. We have all heard stories of Chinese church planters who became translators for Christian organizations, and Chinese seminarians who become immigrants in the West. As Westerners, our financial investment in China has various consequences, both intended and unintended. Many have reiterated is the importance for us Westerners to do our part in our Chinese service; we must embrace a mentality to foster Chinese self-sufficiency, including a clearly defined exit strategy for our organizations' work in China.

We will promote a spirit of unity in the China-concerned Christian community. As we developed these Foundations, we focused greatly on how we treat each other as Westerners serving alongside one another in China. As I shared previously, the issue of working with either the open church or the house church can be divisive, but it should not be. In Ephesians 4, Paul encourages us to 'attain to the unity of the faith,' that all those in Christ serve the same Lord and Savior. We can use biblical principles for conflict resolution when there is a difference in approach, as opposed to disputing our disagreements public.

We should not question others' faith or calling into ministry, even when approaches in China differ. Additionally, we need to have a sense of transparency; we need to draw believers to China so they may see for themselves what God is doing.

We will accurately communicate information for which we have verifiable knowledge. This Foundation is an important one to me, as I've tracked how some organizations portray Christianity in China. From my perception, some Western organizations try to perpetuate the myth that massive persecution of Christians still exists today in China. We feel strongly about the messages we send regarding Christianity in China. As we developed these Foundations, many interesting issues surfaced; some of the most pressing issues we tackled included the need to set up safeguards against an inappropriate inducement of the source of our information, and the need to make sure our information is verifiable through reliable sources.

Since many of our organizations are members of the Evangelical Council for Financial Accountability (ECFA), we've used their standard as a baseline for our own communication about China. ECFA Standard 7.1 states,

> "Narrative about events must be current, complete and accurate. References to past activities or events must be appropriately dated. There must be no material omissions or exaggerations of fact or use of misleading photographs or any other communication which would tend to create a false impression or misunderstanding."[5]

We've heard many stories about organizations that displayed an old, outdated picture, exaggerated the situation in China, or left out important parts of the whole story. This topic is important for two reasons. We accomplish the first Foundation by showing the Chinese government and people that we are using their lack of rule of law for the benefit of our own organizations. We can show the credibility of Christ through truthful communication about their country. Further, by revealing some of the areas opening up in China, we present an accurate picture to the Western Church, inviting them to engage in God's work in China.

New Opportunities for Westerners in China

Through the changes of the last thirty years, God has opened many doors had been previously closed. Westerner newcomers and old-timers alike find many opportunities to join forces to advance God's Kingdom in China; some of these may not have been possible even fifteen years ago. The following are some of the most strategic opportunities:

Bible Distribution

Many westerners embrace the belief that there is an intense need to smuggle Bibles into China to meet the need of

Chinese Christians. While that may have been true twenty years ago, there is no need to smuggle Bibles today; there is now a Chinese organization printing Bibles with the cooperation of Chinese governmental officials. The Chinese organization is called the Amity Printing Company (APC), and it is a cooperative effort between the China Christian Council and the United Bible Societies.

APC's printing facility is located just outside of Nanjing, a city in the central part of Eastern China. APC's General Manager is Li Chunnong, a great guy and the key executive in the Bible printing process. In 2011, over 10 million copies of the Bible were printed at the APC facility, openly and legally. The Bible that is printed at APC is the standard Chinese translation of the Bible, called the Union Version. Best of all, APC's Bibles are legally recognized by the government. As APC staff often tell me, "No recipient in China will ever get into trouble for having an Amity Bible." As the Bibles are produced, they travel by railcar from Nanjing to seventy distribution points to be distributed throughout the country. APC's Bible distribution vans deliver the Bibles to rural and urban areas alike. These vans enable the Bibles to be delivered to places that previously did not receive a regular flow of Bibles. In December 2007, APC opened a new 10-acre Bible Printing plant, which now has the capacity to print over 1 million Bibles each month.

A growing group of Western organizations are seizing the opportunity to print Bibles in China and to engage in Bible distribution. This distribution targets those who cannot afford an Amity Bible, or those who live in very remote, rural locations. These Western organizations have developed relationships with people at United Bible Societies and the China Christian Council, at the local level. One American pastor has developed an organization that has distributed over 200,000 Bibles, as of December 2007. His organization purchases each Bible from Amity and then ships them to the remote location. Once the shipments arrive, the on-site staff ensures that the Bibles arrive in the hands of those who cannot afford them. Between five and ten thousand Bibles are distributed at no cost to each location. This is a wonderfully simple ministry with which any Church in America could get involved. Each Bible costs about $3.00 so it has a big 'bang for your buck.'

Theological Training

With the explosion of Christianity in China, there has been an intense need for trained, qualified leaders to guide the Chinese church into the 21st Century. This is perhaps the greatest need and one of the most important things we can offer the Church in China today. By recruiting Western and Western-based Chinese pastors to go to China for 1- to 2-week trips to train leaders, we give them practical information that they can pass on to others within the Church.

In my own ministry, I hear stories of rural Churches baptizing 2,000 new believers every six months; many of those new believers are asked to lead congregations only three months after conversion. One of the more encouraging trends in this area is the involvement of these Chinese pastors who are pastoring Chinese congregations in the West. Most of them speak Chinese, which eliminates the need for translators. Since they are also Chinese, they understand training from a Chinese perspective, and they provide students with a context that we cannot. This critical ministry needs Anglo and Chinese pastors.

Humanitarian and Social Service

Whether you desire to serve in China's orphanages, provide Christian counseling, or work with governmental officials in areas like humanitarian aid, drought relief or medical assistance, Chinese governmental officials are increasingly willing to partner with us. As with any partnership, an important first step is to go to China to build relationships and listen to their needs.

I encountered this encouraging example in 2003: With the onset of the SARS virus, many in Beijing were scared and afraid of this unknown virus. Chinese people tend to worry more about illness than Westerners do, and in Beijing, the scare level rose to its peak. People stopped going to work or traveling into the city, and Beijing nearly shut down. The Beijing city government needed the citizens to return to work and to the stores. After many late night strategy sessions, they determined to set up counseling centers to educate Beijingers on the SARS virus, to calm the fears that had gripped the city. During one of these sessions, the vice-mayor of Beijing mentioned that an American who lived in his apartment building had a counseling background. The vice-mayor trusted his American friend; they had gotten to know one another as neighbors over the course of two years, and the two families had enjoyed many dinners together. The American who on staff with a large evangelical organization, he had a Master's degree in Counseling, and he was thrilled when the vice-mayor approached and asked him to serve the Beijing government in this way.

In all, they set up thirteen counseling centers in Beijing for the SARS crisis. The counseling was based on Christian principles, which was a tremendous benefit to the city of Beijing; once the SARS crisis ended, they were compelled to keep two of the centers open. One center has a 24-hour counseling hotline, and anyone in China can call for free counseling.

Building Churches

Churches are springing up like wildflowers among the rural areas of China. There are plentiful opportunities for those with a heart for planting, building, and developing churches. By working together with the church and local officials, more foreign organizations sponsor the building of churches. I have heard many unforgettable stories about building churches. In rural Hebei province, an unregistered church group fell under the spell of heretical teaching, which happens with unfortunate regularity in some of China's remote areas. Their leader taught to go out of their village, live in a cave in the nearby hills, and wait for the return of Christ. They were not allowed to eat or drink anything while they waited for His return. After three weeks, a local villager began searching for one of his relatives who had fallen under this false teaching.

What he found shocked him! The people were severely dehydrated, had lost significant weight, and were beginning to lose mental capabilities. When the group returned to the small city, the local governmental officials were intensely worried that something like this could happen to their own people. They resolved to help this band of believers; they determined to provide proper Biblical training and to build them a proper place to meet. Local officials have already bought the land, and they are waiting for someone to help them build the church. When this falls into place, the local Christians of that area will have the facilities they need to prosper.

Teaching Religious Studies Programs at Top Universities

Throughout the last five years, many of the top universities in China have developed Religious Studies or Christian Studies Departments, as an overflow of the nationwide interest in Christianity. A couple of Western organizations continually try to recruit M.A., M.Div., and Ph.D. degreed Westerners to teach at top universities. They need courses like Bible Survey, Christian Philosophy, Biblical Anthropology, Christian Ethics and Comparative Religions. This is such a wonderful opportunity: to be invited to China and to teach for one or two semesters at top universities. The Chinese hold teachers with such high regard, so you would encounter many additional opportunities to share your hope in Christ aside from this teaching position.

Joint Venture Opportunities

With the openness towards Western goods and services, and with the liberalized laws on starting a business, more Westerners are joining together to open new joint venture opportunities. Both sides bring strengths to this partnership, resulting in an approach with great merits. The Chinese partners know the culture, language, and needs of the Chinese people, and the Western partners may have specialized skills that can contribute to the venture's success.

I've seen many of these opportunities work quite well: a language center, a social service office, a full-fledged business, and a joint venture partnership are each wonderful ways to meet Chinese and provide a valuable service in a Chinese city.

An Example of Working with Transparency

I am encouraged to hear of the increasing transparency and openness that Western organizations bring to China. To me, this openness and transparency best reflects the credibility of Christ to a Chinese world that is already suspicious of foreign Christian groups. These individuals and organizations are looking to 'push the envelope' in China; they do not seek to focus on the negatives and differences between Western and Chinese approaches, but instead they ask the question 'What's the most we can do, given the current situation in China?'

There are certainly major challenges for Western organizations in China, but there are also major opportunities for those who are willing to ask this question. For many reasons, I have always highly regarded Evergreen China Service. It has been my privilege to partner together with the

Evergreen staff on a various projects, and they have helped me tremendously. I love their work, their strategy, their staff, and their long-term approach in China. For example, to join the staff with Evergreen is to make a 10-year-to-lifetime commitment. From their website, their mission is clear: "Our purpose is to assist Shanxi and other Chinese provinces by developing public benefit services for the common people, continuing the good works of Peter Torjesen, acknowledging God's gracious calling in our lives, and reflecting the credibility of Christ."

Finn and Sandy Torjesen established Evergreen China in 1993, on the invitation of the Shanxi Executive Vice Governor's Office to continue the work started by Finn's grandfather Peter, who was a Norwegian missionary in the 1930's and 40's. Today, Evergreen China has a number of projects they have developed to benefit the common people of Shanxi. Their main work in China revolves around their agricultural, medical, community development and English programs, which each partner with local government and Christian groups; each one has a great impact in Shanxi province.

Evergreen China's philosophy of ministry and strategy is second to none. Much of this philosophy is outlined in a document called the *Evergreen Compass*. In the *Compass*, they outline their Core Values:

> **Excellence**: Evergreen strives to maintain a high standard of professional excellence in all of our work. We want to give our best.

> **Integrity**: Evergreen wishes to be known as a trustworthy organization. In all situations we endeavor to be honest and forthright, our words matching our actions.

> **Faithfulness**: "Acknowledging God's gracious calling in our lives," we are committed to per-

severing in the work before us, doing so in a way that honors God and His Word and respects all human beings.

Teamwork: We recognize that accountability for work and character is best developed in intentional community. To that end, local and expatriate workers are expected to function as healthy contributing members of a cohesive team.

Local Appropriateness: We acknowledge that effectiveness is a concept that is locally determined. In all that we do, we seek to act and speak in ways that honor the cultural context of the places and people we work with. Emphasizing local appropriateness throughout all aspects of our lives and our work yields greater results and demonstrates respect for the communities in which we serve.

This local appropriateness makes their work so successful. They acknowledge that the founding individuals are not native Chinese, and they seek to make sure that they don't come into China with their own agendas. As they work in China, they focus on questions like this: What do the local Chinese need? How can we meet this need with our time, talents, and resources? The end of their mission statement succinctly states the key to this appropriateness: they want to reflect 'the credibility of Christ.' The Evergreen staff has developed many of these thoughts, and they have passed them along to organizations like my own. I am thankful for their contribution to the larger Christian community in China.

To continue, I am impressed with the model for ministry. Evergreen's Founder, Finn Torjesen, has explained that if God brings expertise in an area of need in Shanxi, they are free to develop that area of service. This philosophy has diversified Evergreen's work in China, and it has established Evergreen's areas of service in ways Finn never could have imagined. But this approach invites God to work in areas of need, as they've offered themselves as a vessel to Him.

One good example of this is the work of Marc De Ruiter, an Evergreen staff in rural Shanxi. Mark, a Dutch agriculturalist, has been in China since 1997, and he has a cheese factory. Mark desire has been to serve by helping rural farmers find ways to sustain their families through agriculture. His Agricultural Training and Demonstration Center (which is primarily a pig raising center) gives farmers a good quality pig, enabling them to start a farm and make a living. The agricultural center has a sow breeding unit, an artificial insemination center, and a training center for rural farmers. The Center provides basic training in pig raising skills, and they act as a low-cost extension service for farmers. With the great success of the Agricultural Center, Marc has developed a new way to help and assist rural farmers.

In their daily life in rural Shanxi, Marc and his wife needed to be creative in making their own food. Isolated from what they knew as the "real world," they were making their own yogurt and bread; Marc decided they should also make their own cheese. This process of learning how to make cheese has been a long one, but as they continued refining the process, they learned that they were good at it. Chinese people don't normally eat cheese, so good cheese is hard to find. Their cheese was pretty good!

As Marc continued to refine the process of making cheese, he brought over cheese makers from Holland; he trained his staff and built proper facilities, creating a small cheese factory called Yellow Valley Cheese. The factory benefits the impoverished farmers in the Shanxi countryside. Marc explained that they buy the milk from small-scale farmers who each have between two and fifteen cows. They also pay them more than the market price, as an incentive to produce quality milk. They are thereby able to sell the cheese to the expatriate communities in China, as well as to hotel chains throughout China, who desire a good source of cheese in China. More information about the Marc's cheese factory can be found at his website, www.CheeseinChina.com.

Practical Applications for Getting Started

If you are interested in getting on board, you may choose to follow these suggestions for engaging with Government officials:

Learn how the system works.

We may be unfamiliar with the Chinese environment, so we must become good learners. Go into China as a learner, and be open to suggestions from Chinese friends. Andrew Kaiser, with Evergreen China Service, jokes that his full-time job is to have lunch with Governmental officials. Of course his job entails many other things as well, but he has a priority to meet with Taiyuan officials; he seeks to learn how their operations work and to then continually ask how Evergreen can serve them to meet the needs in Taiyuan and in Shanxi province.

Don't be afraid of Chinese governmental officials at any level. They're not the enemy!

The Chinese Government views Christians, both Western and Chinese, as a benefit to society. Through multiple conversations with many different people engaging at different levels, we have learned that Chinese leaders are exploring topics like volunteerism and non-profit work to see the benefits of expanding the capabilities in China. We Westerners, with a long history in both areas, have the opportunity to be an asset to the Chinese as they explore these areas.

*Be careful not to put your own agenda before
that of the local Chinese agencies.*

Westerners are often stereotyped as people who come into a 'missions' situation, believing we know all the answers. Although we often have vast ministry experience and training, we must remember that the Chinese are always the experts in their local areas.

When we are willing to set our agendas aside, we invite great cooperation, opening the door for our Chinese partners to ask us for help as needed. We can offer our expertise, but it is on their terms. This type of attitude speaks volumes to our Chinese friends; it demonstrates that we do not simply want to be "in charge."

Final Thoughts

Many people in the West continue to hold on to mental images of the China of fifty years ago. Many still think of China in terms of red guards, Mao Zedong, Cultural Revolution, communal farms and little red books. The China of today is far removed from those images of yesteryear. To think of China with these antiquated images is akin to thinking of America today in terms of poodle skirts, Hopalong Cassidy, the music of the Big Bopper, and school segregation. Today's Chinese cities are glimmering with new buildings, BMW's, and Starbucks coffee shops.

The economic and political changes in China have benefited everyone in society, including those of religious faith. China's rapid economic development has significantly liberalized its political system; this liberalization has also benefited Christians, many of whom are freer to practice their faith than they were at any other time in Chinese history.

Additionally, I've have seen innumerable cases where unregistered and registered Christians, especially among the younger generations, intermingle with each other, looking for ways to work together. We should encourage this intermingling; we can set a positive tone for the reconciliation of the Church in China. On the heels of these changes, God is also providing an unprecedented amount of opportunities for Westerners to work in cooperation with governmental officials at all levels. Persecution of Christians is on the decrease, but that does not mean the task is complete. We must shift our paradigm to find where God is working, where we can serve, and how we can help the existing Church in China.

This is how I define the goal of missions: to plant churches among an indigenous people that is self-supporting, self-governing and self-propagating. We have found that the Church in China is coming close to accomplishing all three of those goals, thanks to the faithful work of foreign Christians over the last 200 years. As the Chinese Church continues to strive to accomplish those goals, we have two options: we can help them become a self-governing, propagating and supporting church, or we can continue to control them for our own benefit. Our ministry should be so effective that the Church in China will eventually no longer need us.

In my opinion, we would be wise to follow the advice of a Beijing house church pastor, interviewed by Luis Palau during his April 2004 trip to China. This pastor oversees eight house churches; he told Luis, "Christians in America need to get over their insatiable hunger for persecution stories, and we in the house churches must get over our persecution complex. Yes, there has been persecution in this city's past, but our greatest need is not eliminating persecution, but building up mature fellowship and developing unity among Christians."

Read carefully what the Church in China is telling us: 'Get over your incredible desire of persecution stories. That should not be the main focus. We want to build up and disciple mature believers to be unifiers of the Church in China. God has given us a unique opportunity to be involved in the greatest Christian movement in history. Just as Jesus never said a word against the Roman government of His day, we too can embrace the opportunities before us in a new light.

[1] Aikman, David. *Jesus in Beijing: How Christianity Is Transforming China and Changing the Global Balance of Power*. Washington, D.C. Regnery Publishing. 2003.
[2] Burklin, Werner. *Jesus never left China*. Enumclaw, WA. Pleasant Word. 2005
[3] Hutzler, Charles, "Mixing Religion and Noodles Lands Ms. Su in Hot Water," June 2, 2005, *Wall Street Journal*.
[4] Crosswalk. "Matthew Henry Complete Commentary on the Whole Bible." [Online] March 31, 2008. <http://bible.crosswalk.com/Commentaries/Matthew HenryComplete/mhc.com.cgi?book=ro&chapter=13#Ro13_1>
[5] Evangelical Council for Financial Accountability. "Seven Standards for Responsible Stewardship." [Online] March 1, 2008. <http://www.ecfa.org/Content.aspx? PageName=7Standards>

Chapter 7

China's Other People: The Ethnic Minorities

> And they sang a new song, saying, "Worthy are you to take the scroll and to open its seals, for you were slain, and by your blood you ransomed people for God from every tribe and language and people and nation, and you have made them a kingdom and priests to our God, and they shall reign on the earth."
> —*Revelation 5:9-10 (ESV)*

When most of us think of Chinese people, we hold a stereotypical picture in our minds about what someone from China looks like—olive skin, almond-shaped eyes, and straight black hair. In reality, that stereotype represents only a portion of the total population in China. The vast territory of China encompasses many different cultures, people groups, and races, from pale, blue-eyed peoples to nomadic hunters to jungle-dwelling tribal members. While the Han people comprise 91% of China's population, they represent only one of 56 officially recognized people groups in China. Differences exist even within the Han culture. The farmers of the Yellow River basin are distinct from those of the Yangtze, who are themselves different from those in China's northeast region. Dialects of Mandarin Chinese differ from one area of China to another, and in areas populated by ethnic minority groups, one does not have to go far to encounter a completely different language. Not counting the Han, the 55 other people groups living in China add 115 million to the population total.

This chapter will explain how the Chinese government conveniently combines 450 minority groups into just 56 ethnic classifications. In addition, I hope to provide a broad overview of the culture and history of these varying people groups, including a glimpse into God's work in their lives. On a side note, the material in this chapter is the result of direct feedback I've received from those who are using the book to train staff for ministry in China. I certainly hope it helps!

Finding the Hidden Peoples

For centuries, outsiders knew little about the ethnic minorities in China. The practical and geographical barriers that separated Han populations from ethnic minority groups kept many secondary cultures hidden from the outside world. Even Chinese scholars of the 18th and 19th centuries were not motivated to examine subcultural groups in their own society. Han researchers had little to no interest in studying these people groups prior to 1950. A 'Han-centric' way of thinking stemmed from the royal belief that any groups outside imperial rule were to be regarded as wholly separate cultures. The Communist takeover of China in 1949 reflected a Soviet-style approach to minority groups. Nations were defined as people who shared a common language, history, culture and territory. According to the Soviet model, each people group, or nation, that shared these commonalities had the right to secede from a larger federated government.

The huge number of ethnicities residing in China's territories proved quite inconvenient in regard to the Soviet view of minority groups. Even so, China adopted the policies of the neighboring USSR in terms of minorities, except that minority groups were never given the right to secede. Instead, the People's Republic transformed China into a "multi-national state," identifying traditional minority groups as 'nationalities.' Each such group began nurturing its own sense of nationalism.

Governmental awareness and understanding of minority groups began to grow in the 1950's as the government, wanting to extend their reach to all parts of China, started massive construction projects of roads and rail. Remote villages that once required a very difficult journey on foot or by horse became a much shorter trip by air or car from the nearest provincial capital. Perhaps most importantly, the Communist Party made Mandarin Chinese the national language, dictating that it be taught in schools and used for business throughout the country. Minority group members who at one time had no way to communicate with their Han countrymen could now discuss common issues with them. Researchers began to gather more accurate information about minorities, especially previously unknown groups.

At the drafting of the 1954 Chinese constitution, the government invited leaders from the various minority groups throughout China to register for official recognition. Much to the government's surprise, over 400 groups submitted applications for acknowledgement. Under the Stalinist model that the Chinese government initially used, each of these 400 groups would have official representation with the Chinese government and would retain the right to eventually secede from China and form their own country. Later, however, the government proved unwilling to deal individually with such a large number of groups, and attempted to shrink the list to a more manageable size. To address the huge volume of applications, the government sent teams of experts out to investigate each people group; the list was narrowed from 400 to 183. Using that list and a formula that combined similar ethnicities, the list of groups dropped to a total of 56.

While a shorter list of China's people groups may have been convenient for the Central government, the 56 minority designations failed to adequately or accurately represent China's ethnic minorities. Some minority group leaders were upset about being merged with other groups. Paul Hattaway's excellent book, *Operation China*, relates one poignant story: "The small Lopi people group who live on the Yunnan-Sichuan border have been officially included as part of [the] Yi minority group, but 'they think of the Yi as mountain barbarians and have no wish to be associated with them; they are both puzzled and bitter that they have not won recognition as a separate nationality.'"[1] I strongly recommend Mr. Hattaway's book for those who have an interest in learning more about each of the 400 ethnic minorities.

Policy + Tibet + Xinjiang = Unanticipated Results

More than 80 percent of Chinese who lack sufficient food and clothing live in minority areas. Governmental leaders continue to insist that ethic unity can be established only when the standard of living in minority areas is greatly improved. As the Chinese government's awareness of ethnic minorities has grown, they have instituted policies designed to improve living conditions among these populations. Article 122 of PRC's constitution states, "The state provides financial, material and technical assistance to the minority nationalities to accelerate their economic and cultural development." These state-sponsored, preferential policies favor minorities in a number of areas and are among the world's oldest and largest subsidy programs of their kind. The Central government has introduced many favorable polices toward minorities and provided huge financial subsidies to autonomous regions. In 1984, the Chinese courts were ordered to reduce criminal charges and penalties imposed on minority suspects. By 2016, Beijing plans to invest $21.7 billion (US) in Tibet. University admissions, family planning, administrative positions in autonomous areas, and dual language school systems for local minorities are some of the key preferential policies that have been implemented throughout China. While the long-term effects of these policies are yet to be seen, the policies, enacted under a dominant Han society, are affecting the stability in some minority regions.

The Tibetan and Uighur (pronounced *wee-gur*) people groups make up two of the larger minorities in China. Both occupy an autonomous region, politically separated from the other provinces. These autonomous regions, while still influenced by the Central government, have significant legislative authority and the ability to appoint governors from their own ethnicities. The Tibet Autonomous Region lies in southwestern China. Xinjiang Autonomous Region, designated for the Uighurs, is located in northwestern China. Despite certain positive effects of preferential policies instituted by the Central government, other factors pose challenges to long-term stability in both Tibet and Xinjiang. Recently, populations in both regions have been involved in rioting and unrest, earning a fair amount of coverage in the international press.

With encouragement from the Central government, Han Chinese have migrated to areas in Tibet, Xinjiang and other regions populated by minority groups. Such moves have served two functions: the Central government is better able to maintain political control and monitor public safety in these areas, and Han entrepreneurs have been able to pursue new economic opportunities. Generally, Han migrants bring cash and government connections to the local economies. Minority groups generally don't fare as well. The economic realities in China are such that despite preferential policies granted to minority populations, these people still lack equal access to money-making or educational opportunities, even in their local areas.

The transformation from a centrally planned economy to a market economy over the past three decades has radically altered the situation. Since the official language throughout China is Mandarin Chinese, Han migrants enjoy certain advantages over local minorities. For example, while minority groups may be granted protected access to further education, their lower examination scores dictate the type of schooling they receive. These lower scores are mainly a result of their inability to speak, read and write Mandarin Chinese as well as their Han competitors. Consequently, minority students often find it hard to secure good jobs after graduation. This combination of factors has led to a situation in Tibet and Xinjiang where the benefit of belonging to the local, majority ethnic group has been largely erased, thereby causing ongoing tension in these areas of China.

In March 2008, perceived inequalities boiled over into the streets of Lhasa, Tibet's capital city. Protestors took to the streets, targeting Han-owned businesses in a clear statement of anger about the economic marginalization of native Tibetans. Many in the Western media pointed to the Chinese government as the source of the problem, reporting on governmental 'persecution' of Tibetans. James Miles, a reporter with the Economist magazine, witnessed the riots but insisted that police presence during the Lhasa riots was calm and even-handed: "What I saw was calculated, targeted violence against an ethnic group, or I should say two ethnic groups, primarily ethnic Han Chinese living in Lhasa."[2]

The second ethnic group to which Miles was referring was the Hui people, who tended to identify with the Han Chinese. Miles' eyewitness account contradicted general news reports that indicated the Chinese police brutally attacked native Tibetans. He claimed the reverse: native Tibetans were specifically directing their outrage against the Han and Hui peoples. In July 2009, Xinjiang's capital city, Urumqi, saw similar protests, which rapidly grew into violent attacks against Han targets. Unlike the Lhasa uprising, in Urumqi the Han population retaliated against Uighurs. By the end of the rioting, 184 people had perished, 137 of whom were Han.

The Chinese government has no easy solutions to their dilemma in Xinjiang and Tibet. Both situations were aggravated by tensions between Han immigrants and the native populations; these tensions stemmed from governmental promotions of nationalism in response to weakening Communist ideology.

Today, Chinese nationalism has adopted a tone of Han supremacy, which is quite alienating to minority peoples who feel no real bond or sense of belonging to Han Chinese civilization. It will be interesting to see the direction Beijing will take in regard to these ethnic minority groups; they may grant more independence to the autonomous regions, or they may attempt to forcibly assimilate local cultures to the Han model. This latter option would likely serve to bring even more unwanted international attention to these regions.

Christian Work Among the Minorities

I have previously described the massive Christian growth that is taking place in China, with millions of Chinese coming to know Christ annually. We praise God for the work that He is clearly doing in China, the vast majority of which is being done amongst the Han in the eastern half of the country. The missionary work that is taking place in ethnic minority areas is, however, a more difficult assignment, with less fruit being produced. One organization that is diving headlong into ministry among lesser recognized people groups in China is Minorities for Christ International. They are based in Sunnyvale, California. Hadul Tamabima, a Taiwanese ethic minority member, started the ministry in 2005; he has proven very helpful to me in my understanding of China's minority groups. Currently, the group's work is focused primarily in the southern half of China where many minority groups live. Eight full-time missionaries, members of ethnic minorities themselves, have planted at least twenty self-supporting sister churches who are themselves eager to plant additional churches.

For the last twelve years, Minorities for Christ International has operated a training center where they've equipped hundreds of native missionaries to work in the minority areas of China. Hadul told an interesting story about how the training center started: "At first we trained Han Chinese to go into these areas. [This] took longer because they still needed cross-cultural training since Han culture and local minority cultures are so different. Now we train local minority Christians to go as missionaries."

He gave the example of Lisu Christians living in Yunnan Province, which borders Tibet. The Lisu language and culture is similar to Tibetan, with parts of the language being identical; such similarities significantly shorten the training time and allow missionaries to launch their ministries much sooner. Minorities for Christ International now has hundreds of native missionaries operating in China.

When I asked Hadul what challenges these missionaries face, he told me that their number one difficulty is that some of the minority groups they seek to reach regularly cross Chinese borders; they may move back and forth between China and Northern Vietnam, Northern Laos or India. Missionaries must seek official approval to cross back and forth between borders to work with these groups. Workers in south China face a different challenge, where residents of remote jungle villages are extremely difficult to reach. I asked Hadul about access to Bibles in the areas where they work, since I had heard stories of people in south China not having a copy of the Bible in their 'heart' language. Access to native language Bibles varies; Hadul reported that some minority people have a Bible in their language and some do not. Most young people can read Mandarin Chinese since it's taught in every school in China, and so they often read Bibles written in this language with little or no difficulty. Hadul did tell me that 80% of the older people cannot read Mandarin and consequently do not have a Bible written in their native language.

Praise God for the work being done amongst China's ethnic minority groups! Unfortunately, there are far too few Christians like Hadul who are targeting these people groups with the Gospel. I pray for more workers in these difficult mission fields. Revelation describes a wonderful scene of worshipers, all of whom have been saved by the blood of Christ and who come from 'every tribe and language and people and nation.' How I look forward to seeing each and every people group in China represented at this worship service!

Dry Ground and Thorns Among the Ethnic Minorities

One of the most difficult aspects of an overview like this one is that such diversity of language, culture and religious traditions between ethnic minorities makes summarizing their beliefs seem an impossible task. Looking at general trends within China's ethnic minorities, however, certain patterns do emerge as Christians seek to impact these people groups for Christ.

Ancestor worship has been a longstanding tradition among many Asian cultures; it is practiced in some form by almost every community and people group in China. Generally defined, the Asian-style of ancestor worship seeks to honor the deeds and the memories of the deceased. Paying filial respect to deceased parents and other family elders is thought to ensure their well-being; in turn, many adherents believe that ancestors influence the fortunes of the living. In

China, ancestor worship is practiced by many ethnic groups, including the Han. For most adherents, it represents a main feature of their religious beliefs and practices, keeping them in bondage to the past and preventing them from receiving Christ. It would be an insult to their ancestors to turn away from tradition and acknowledge a Savior.

Ancestor worship can also be a financial burden on minority families. Stories are told, for example, of poor families who don't want an ancestor involved in a family dispute. They will dig up the grave of the family member and find another burial site to ensure the ancestor's peace and rest. Reburial costs are expensive and impose a huge financial burden on the family. Miao ethnic minorities hold a ceremony every thirteen years to honor ancestors. This ritual includes the sacrificing of a bull, also a costly burden on the family.

In addition to ancestor worship, many minority groups practice a complex mixture of idol worship, animism and polytheism. Within this religious mix, many groups attempt to placate a wide array of spirits and deities. For example, the Nasu people of Yunnan province believe "everything in this world has a soul and… all ghosts are incarnations of human souls. They respect the good and hate the evil. Whenever someone dies a natural death they invite a shaman to pacify the souls of the deceased and send it to the midst of their ancestors."[3]

The Yao people, 2.7 million of whom live in south central and southwest regions of China, represent another example of the spiritual bondage that hinders people from receiving the Gospel. They are a polytheistic society, worshipping a mountain god, an earth god, and practicing ancestor worship. In the formal room of every Yao family is an ancestral tablet seat. During holidays and festivals, they offer gifts and foods to their ancestors. These worship events often include calling family members to meet at the graves of dead relatives to pour rice wine on the burial site.

Sadly, very few Nasu or ethnic Yao have ever heard the name of Jesus. May we all pray that God would similarly move among China's ethnic minorities as He has among the Han!

[1] Hattaway, Paul. *Operation China*. Carlisle, UK. Piquant. 2000
[2] http://edition.cnn.com/2008/WORLD/asiapcf/03/20/tibet.miles.interview/
[3] Kang Enda. "The Yi Minority's Naked Leopard Dance," China Tourism, no. 172 (November 1994).

Chapter 8

How the Chinese View Life, Their Government, and Democracy

"To China's problems, the overwhelming priority is stability. Without a stable environment, nothing can be achieved, and what has been achieved will be lost... Democracy is our goal, but the country must remain stable."

— *Deng Xiaoping, late leader of the Communist Party of China*

One of the greatest pleasures I receive from my work with the China Resource Center is my firsthand involvement with modern-day China. As a student of Chinese history, I am fascinated to be able to study the rapid changes of the last thirty years and then to see the results of those changes. As I have tried to develop a picture of the lives of modern-day

Chinese, I knew from the start that the task would be difficult for a number of reasons. China is so vast, both in area and in population. China has fifty-six different recognized people groups, and each group's situation is unique. There is also a growing divide between the rich and poor in China, mainly divided along urban and rural lines; each of these groups deals with special challenges. There are also Christian and non-Christian, private sector and government officials.... the list goes on and on. But as I talk with Americans about China, it's also clear that people's thoughts and perceptions about the lives of today's Chinese are inaccurate. In painting with very broad strokes, I hope to present useful information to clarify the overall picture of how people in the West see China today.

One of the greatest misperceptions about the Chinese people is that they live horrible lives under a fascist dictator. Nothing could be further from the truth. Westerners assume that we must come in and save the Chinese from the evil Communist dictators. In reality, studies in China continually show that the general population in China is not clamoring for democracy, and they are generally happy with their quality of life. In July 2011, *Pew Global Attitudes* conducted a survey comprising a broad spectrum of Chinese society; 85% of Chinese said the national government has a very good or somewhat good influence on the way things are going in the country.[1] In the same survey, 72% of Chinese were satisfied with national conditions, as opposed to only 39% of Americans who were satisfied with national conditions. In living in China, one can actually find evidence of this satisfaction spilling out in many sectors of the nation. The Chinese love their country, and they are a very patriotic people. They are proud of the nation and its recent accomplishments, and they speak with pride about the growing influence of China on the world stage. So that I may shed additional light on the state of the Chinese people, I must first look back at the enormous changes of the last thirty years in China.

Defining the Change of the Last Three Decades

To understand the depth of the changes that have happened over the last three decades, we must first look at the devastation that took place in China during The Cultural Revolution of 1966 to 1976. Once we truly understand the degree of China's devastation in 1976, we can fully recognize how rapid the changes have been since then.

Technically known as The Great Proletarian Cultural Revolution, and launched by Mao Zedong, the then-Chairman of the Communist Party of China, it was his last desperate attempt to revive a dying revolution. It was a method to regain control of the party after a significant loss of power to Mao's political rivals in the years preceding 1966. Mao's great Communist revolution was not unfolding as he had envisioned, and after conceding power to several others in 1960, Mao spent a number of years studying political economy and the classics of Chinese history. Mao was unhappy with the revisionist direction that the Communist party was taking, and he determined to take action. Gathering a group of Mao loyalists and his principal lieutenants, called the Red Guards, they attacked the new leadership of the Chinese Communist party; Mao hoped to seize control of the state and party apparatus. In the violence and chaos that ensued, many elders of the earlier revolution, authors, artists and religious figures were purged, persecuted or killed, all in an attempt to wipe clean the establishment set by the previous 4,000 years of China's history. Mao optimistically proclaimed that China was a 'clean sheet of paper.' Anyone who wore western clothing, professed a religion, or had a college education was persecuted. Young intellectuals from the cities were forcibly moved to the rural areas to work as farm labor and study Communist propaganda. Tilling the land and living a Spartan life was the chosen path to cure them of their intellect. In the same way, many Party officials were forced to move, thereby abolishing their bureaucratic habits. In addition, many cultural and historical relics were destroyed in an attempt to purge China from its imperial past. The Cultural Revolution was a failure in every imaginable way, and it led to horrific devastation in China and among the Chinese people. Estimates on the human toll of the Cultural Revolution are varied, but some accounts estimate that over 500,000 people were killed.

At the conclusion of the Revolution, the Chinese economy was a complete mess. With the political succession of Deng Xiaoping as 'paramount leader' of the Chinese Communist Party in 1978, Deng initiated measures to liberalize the economy and release the grip of the government on China's population. He also set out to re-establish relations overseas, traveling on a number of international goodwill trips during the late 1970's. Deng set out to reduce the role of ideology in the decisions of the economy, in favor of establishing policies of proven effectiveness. With the launch of the 'Four Modernizations,' modernizing the fields of Agriculture, Industry, Science and Technology, and the Military, Deng intended to develop China into a great economic power by the early 21st century. These reforms stressed economic self-reliance, and they were designed to accelerate the modernization process and economic development by opening up China's markets and pursuing foreign investment.

Looking back on Deng's reforms with our 21st Century perspective, we can confidently see the success of his revitalization plan. An analysis of the last thirty five years' growth in China could fill many more pages in this book, but several key examples state the case. In 1977, China's exports to the world market totaled about $63 million dollars; in 2011 that amount had grown to $1.89 trillion dollars, a 25.9 percent increase from a year earlier. And according to the New York Times, the Chinese economy should surpass the U.S. economy by the year 2027.[2] Since the market reforms of the early 1980's, China's economy has shown 10% growth each year, with the growth rate reaching 12-15% through the first seven years of the 21st century. In 2011, China's economy grew by nearly 10% to become the second largest economy in the world. (To put this growth into perspective, the United States economy grew 1.7% in 2011.) In 1977, China's business and manufacturing sectors were completely state-run, and the private sector was non-existent. By contrast, the private sector contributed 60% of China's annual GDP in 2011. In fact, an examination of current economic trends in China indicates that state-run businesses have almost completely fallen out of competitive sectors of the Chinese economy, because they can't compete with the private sector. In 1977, there were 310,000 college students in China; in 2007, there are 5.9 million and today there are over 20 million. In 1977, Chinese, government officials were all rank and file Communist party members, with no job experience outside of the party. In 2011, more than half of the Chinese governmental officials had private sector experience.

In the process of this remarkable economic growth, Chinese lawmakers have crafted the first sets of laws in Chinese history. Because the Mao Zedong era was ruled essentially as a police-state, many Chinese had no understanding of law or a set of laws that governs the country. Several of my Chinese friends have told me they grew up in the 1950's and 1960's with no concept of law; even the word 'law' was extremely foreign to them. For this generation of Chinese, lawyers and attorneys were relegated to the history books, and many didn't even know that such a profession existed. One friend told me recently, "The first time I ever heard of a law was when I saw the term on my marriage certificate in 1982. I had to ask my wife what that word meant."

In July 1979, the Chinese government developed its first Criminal Law, borrowing heavily from Soviet scholarship and legal experience. The 1979 Criminal Law was heavily flawed and would not be revised until 1997. In 1982, China's first Business Law was established, as well as a set of laws dealing with foreign businesses. These laws were significant, because they set a standard for business in China and overseas. In 1986, General Principles of Civic Laws were first published and went into effect the following year. These laws were to create a consistent framework for the interpretation of civil law in China. 1986 was the first year that they first defined a *human being*. In the 1990's, we see additional precedents in the area of law: the 1995 State Compensation Law, the 1997 revision of the Criminal Law, Premier Zhu Rongji in 1998, exclaiming that China should be ruled by law, and the 1999 Contract Law. In addition to amazing economic growth, we also see the development of the idea of law during the last thirty-five years, which then led to the 'rule of law', examined in Chapter 2. This period of Chinese history is important for us to understand, because it shows us China's youth and freshness in the area of 'rule of law.' We can almost view China as a new country, even though their history extends for 5,000 years. All of the Chinese laws have emerged within the last thirty years.

Democracy in China

One of the West's criticisms of China is the lack of people's participation in government in a democratic form. Many Westerners see this lack of democracy in China as a deficiency to remedy. Contrary to popular belief in the West, most Chinese do not see the development of democracy as one of their nation's top needs of the future. Much of the Chinese population embraces the belief that their current government effectively meets the country's needs.

They root this belief in three main reasons. First, many Chinese prioritize the continuation of massive development of the country's infrastructure and the effort to bridge the gap between the standards of urban and rural living. A plunge into potential political chaos would hinder the development of the country. Secondly, many Chinese do not yet know much about democracy or the democratic process, so the concept is unclear to them. China does not have a history of multi-party democracy, and intellectuals are overwhelmingly in favor of slow steps of progress toward political reform. Thirdly, they understand their current political system, and generally, they are living great lives under the current regime. People in the cities are making money, driving cars, dining at the Outback Steakhouse on Saturday night, traveling overseas, seeing new destinations, buying real estate, purchasing new consumer electronics (such as flat-screen TV's, DVD players, and stereo systems) for their real estate, and buying the latest fashions. They are living well. It is my overwhelming impression that they are too busy making money to press for much political change; they see no need to change something that isn't broken. Remember the survey from earlier in the chapter: 85% of Chinese approve of the performance of the Chinese government. It seems to me that only deep, widespread dissatisfaction with the current government would lead to any changes.

Within this high rate of satisfaction among the Chinese population, there are some interesting and theoretical rumblings taking place amongst intellectuals and political leaders about democracy. In February 2007, Xie Tao, a retired Vice President of Beijing's Renmin University, published an article in the Chinese monthly journal, *Yanhuang Chunqiu*. He praised Sweden's Social Democratic Party as a model for China's Communist Party. Mr. Xie did not explicitly mention a multi-party system, but he scorned the Communist party's continued stance on the 'utopian' ideal of communism. Swift reactions followed the article, and camps on both sides of the issue appeared. Official state newspapers, like the *People's Daily*, criticized European-style social democracy as inappropriate for China. Professor Zheng Yongnian, the head of research at the China Policy Institute of The University of Nottingham, states, "After Xie Tao's article appeared, clearly defined for—and against-camps sprang up, but the official response was ambiguous. Even those official scholars who said social democracy was not suited to China's needs acknowledged that social democracy has much to offer."[3]

A major reason that many intellectuals and government leaders in China may be drawn towards a social democratic model is that social democrats aim to reform capitalism democratically through state regulation. They also favor the creation of state-sponsored programs and organizations, which work to improve or remove injustices purportedly inflicted by the capitalist market system. Social democracy normally has an extensive system of social security (which is already in place in China) and a government system that regulates private enterprise in the interest of workers, consumers and fair competition. Professor Zheng continued, "Many Chinese who visit Europe these days are left with a strong impression of European-style social democracy, and many of them can see from the European model the ideal society that many generations of Chinese were pursuing. In dealing with the many social problems that China faces, such as environmental degradation, excessive income disparities, the loss of social harmony, etc., people can look for useful experiences in Europe."[4]

There are also those within the Chinese government weighing in on the Social Democracy debate. Zhou Tianyong, a senior official at the Central Party School, was the lead writer for a lengthy article on Social Democracy in China, written in the *Review of Economic Research*, a journal run by China's Ministry of Finance. The authors concluded that the transition to a Social Democracy could be achieved over the next twenty years. China's President has also made some waves with comments he's about political reform in China. Within the last year, he has tolerated an unusual amount of open debate about China's political options. Calls for multi-party democracy remain off the table, but that seems to be the one restriction. In a highly publicized speech in June 2007, Hu said that the changes to China's political structure over the last three decades had proceeded in an 'active and prudent way,' and without democracy there could be no continual modernization of China.

Taiwan on my Mind

Another issue that garners confusion in the minds of many in the West is the issue of Taiwan and its role with China. It is easy to see why there is so much confusion. A little history lesson may help clarify this situation.

The current government of Taiwan, the Republic of China (ROC), was established in 1912, replacing the Qing Dynasty as the governmental authority over much of what we would consider China today. Under the leadership of Chiang Kai-Shek, the ROC lost the civil war with the Chinese Communist Party, and the ROC government had to flee to the island of Taiwan. With its governmental capital in Taipei, the ROC still formally claims to be the government over all of China; the current Communist government in Mainland China is the government for the People's Republic of China (PRC), and it views the ROC as illegitimate. The PRC also sees Taiwan as a renegade province of mainland China. Viewing themselves as a sovereign and independent country, the ROC has not seen the need for a formal declaration of independence. Interestingly, during the period of PRC isolation during the middle three decades of the 20th century, the United States had formal diplomatic relations with the ROC government as its representative of China. During the 1976 reopening of the PRC to the West, the United States dropped its formal relationship with the ROC in favor of diplomatic relations with the PRC. Today, the ROC is a thriving democratic society of over 23 million people. Its status in the world is very dependent on whom you ask. In the West, we easily view Taiwan as an independent country, worthy of full recognition of national status. With a democratically-elected government as well as a full and independent banking and monetary system, Taiwan operates just like any other government around the world.

But to the Chinese, the situation looks quite different. It would be understandable to learn that PRC governmental officials see Taiwan as a renegade province; they could look forward and expect eventual reunification with Taiwan, under Chinese governmental control. What has surprised me a bit is to hear this from everyday Chinese, including my Chinese friends studying at American universities and Christian friends in China. Throughout all of China, cries for eventual reconnection with Taiwan invade all sectors of society. This is fascinating to me, since it seems quite clear that Taiwan bears all the indicators of a sovereign nation, from my perspective. But for the Chinese, there is much more than what meets the eye. Many of them see their own Han Chinese people living in Taiwan; more specifically, many of them have family members who fled to Taiwan Island. For the Mainland Chinese with the surname Li, they know of Li family members who are in Taiwan. They look at Taiwan as they look at themselves; they would say, "That is us over there." This causes the Mainland Chinese to be so persistent in their view of Taiwan.

Despite all the satisfaction that the Chinese people feel about their government, all is not well with the Chinese government. A couple of important issues surface regularly: the corruption of governmental officials, and the inequality of income distribution between urban and rural segments of society.

Corruption in the Government

In China today, corruption within the ranks of government leaders is endemic; it is the greatest threat to the Communist Party's continued hold on power. By its own admission, bribery, extortion, smuggling and racketeering are pervasive throughout every level of the Communist Party. Without firm action, many in the Chinese government fear that ordinary Chinese will lose faith in the Party. Public opinion surveys in China repeatedly identify corruption as one of the public's top concerns. The most common accusations are toward officials, who are at the center of decision making in their local economy, abusing their position to extract bribes and kickbacks, with little or no established accountability to halt such crimes.

Remember what I've already written about the development of rule of law in China: the root problem is the lack of separation between business and government under the 'Socialist Market Economy.' Seeing corruption as a serious political liability, the Chinese Government has spent billions to crack down on what they see as a 'social pollution' that threatens the state of the nation. According to a 2006 *Washington Post* article,[5] the Chinese Communist Party disciplined more than 123,000 members for corruption and related violations last year, and they turned more than 15,000 of them over to the courts for prosecution.

Rural vs. Urban Divide Getting Wider

In modern-day China, the gap between the rich and the poor continues to widen, causing concern not only for international China watchers, but also for the Chinese government themselves. Despite having the world's fastest-growing economy, it also has one of its most unequal societies. Once a stalwart of the Communist Party, the 710 million peasants in China have been quickly left behind, as the benefits of growth go mostly to urban residents. The main reason for this growing disparity rests in the policies the government made when they underwent economic reforms, from a planned economy to a market economy. One of Deng Xiaoping's Four Modernizations was the rapid increase of industrialization, which also meant urbanization. More of the resources flowed into building up industry, and when industrialization brought money, the profits stayed in the cities. As a result, many of today's farmers flock to the cities of China, looking for work so they can send money back to the family that stays behind.

Here is a good way to numerically describe what is happening with this divide. The Gini coefficient is an international standard to measure the inequality of income distribution between the poorest and richest populations in any given nation. It is defined as a ratio, with values between 0 and 1. A low Gini coefficient indicates more equal income distribution, and a high Gini coefficient indicates more unequal distribution. Therefore, a Gini coefficient of 0 means that everyone has exactly the same income. In 1964, 90% of China's population lived in rural areas, with a Gini of .18. By 1981, 80% of China's population inhabited the rural areas, and the Gini had changed to .26. Today, only 55% of the population lives in rural areas, and the Gini has grown to .42. The internationally recognized warning line for a nation's Gini coefficient is .4. China is in the bottom 20% of a ranking of the nations of the world in their Gini coefficient, which has sparked widespread concern over the inequality of income distribution.

Whenever I think about this growing disparity, I quickly recall my growing experiences in the rural areas of China. Whenever I'm in China, I always love to get out of the cities and into the rural area. With my work in China, most of our projects aim to serve rural Christians, because God seems to be most at work in the rural areas, and because those who live in these rural areas could not otherwise afford the services we provide. The Christians in these areas are so full of peace and joy in the midst of their financial status, which puts a new spin on Gini coefficients and technical statistics. On one hand, I am always struck by the lack of basic infrastructure and public services. When we do rural Bible distribution for example, we carry the Bibles in vans out into the areas where they need them most. As we leave our 'base camp' in the city early in the morning, the roads on which we travel continue to get worse. We go from paved highway to paved local road, then we travel on a dirt road, and many times we carrying the boxes of Bibles in our hands for the last mile to the distribution site, since the roads are inaccessible by car. On the other hand, it seems that in those rural populations, the material insufficiencies are somewhat immaterial. They seem to have determined in their own minds, "I have Christ, and He's all I really need!"

As I travel to these areas to administer our projects, I love two things the most. First, I love the fire and zeal these rural Christians have for Christ. Their passion is so contagious! I've told friends that if I could convince my wife to live in one of these very remote areas, then we would learn as much from them as they would learn from us. They pray fervently for Christ to come mightily on China, and they evangelize like the Lord is coming back tomorrow. There is so much to love about these friends. I also love and admire their zeal in spite of their financial condition. I've personally talked with rural Christians who are making the equivalent of $4.00 US a month, yet they don't seem to mind.

One of my greatest privileges is to spend time with these rural Christians. They represent the best of what Christ has to offer China and the Chinese people. With Christ, Communism doesn't seem as bad. With Christ, lack of democracy isn't a big concern. These people are the reason I am involved in China. My greatest desire is to bring China to Christ, so that no matter what the future holds, the Chinese people will have Christ. He is all they need.

[1] Pew Research Center. http://www.pewglobal.org/database/?indicator=3&country=45
[2] http://articles.economictimes.indiatimes.com/2011-12-12/news/30505077_1_euro-crisis-india-and-china-euro-collapse
[3] The University of Nottingham, China Policy Institute. "Yongnian_Zheng_Zaobao_Column_16th_Oct_2007." [Online] October 19, 2007. <http://www.nottingham.ac.uk/china-policy-institute/china/documents/Yongnian_Zheng_Zaobao_Column_16th_Oct._2007.pdf>
[4] The University of Nottingham, China Policy Institute. "Yongnian_Zheng_Zaobao_Column_16th_Oct_2007." [Online] October 19, 2007. <http://www.nottingham.ac.uk/china-policy-institute/china/documents/Yongnian_Zheng_Zaobao_Column_16th_Oct._2007.pdf>
[5] Washington Post. "China Cracks Down on Corruption." [Online] February 15, 2006.< http://www.washingtonpost.com/wp-dyn /content/article/2006/02/14/AR2006021400672.html>

Chapter 9

About China Resource Center—God's Divine Calling Into His Work

"I believe God made me for a purpose, but he also made me fast. And when I run I feel His pleasure."
—*Eric Liddell*, Chariots of Fire

"Don't ask yourself what the world needs. Ask yourself what makes you come alive and then go do that. Because what the world needs is people who have come alive."
—*Howard Thurman*

One of my favorite movies of all time is *Chariots of Fire*, the 1981 British film based on the true story of two British athletes competing in the 1924 Paris Summer Olympics. One of those athletes was Eric Liddell, a Scotsman born in Tianjin, China to missionary parents. My favorite scene in the movie is when Eric has a conversation with his sister, who is concerned that Eric's running is taking him away from the family's China mission. To reassure his sister, he tells her that God had given him certain gifts and abilities. When Eric ran, he knew that God was smiling.

Have you ever felt God's pleasure in that way? If you have, then you know what Eric is talking about. It is a feeling like none other available to us on this side of Heaven. When I'm in China, using the Chinese language with Chinese people, I feel God's pleasure. It's like God is saying: "Mike, this is what I made you to do." My heart feels full. I feel no lack or absence of anything in those situations. I am the created one, fulfilling the purpose of the Creator.

Over the years, God has led me many times to a very familiar verse. Psalm 37:3-5 says, 'Trust in the Lord, and do good; dwell in the land and befriend faithfulness. Delight yourself in the Lord, and He will give you the desires of your heart. Commit your way to the Lord; trust in Him, and he will act." I love the idea that as we delight in who God is, as we meditate on Him, He will give us the desires of our hearts. I've found that He does not necessarily give us the fancy sports car or the big house we may want, but His desires become our desires. He actually replaces our selfish desires with His holy desires. Every time a Western friend comes with me to China to observe one of our projects, each one inevitably tells me the same thing: "Mike, it's clear that you were made for this." I'm not doing anything to impress them or to show off, but when I serve as He made me to serve, I think God's desires just come shining through.

One of the ironic things about my heart for China is that I'm really tall; in fact I'm 6'7" (2 meters), which is a stark contrast from the shorter stature of many Chinese. But it's clear that this is what God wants me to do. I love adventure.

I'm definitely a risk taker. I love Chinese food, I don't mind the dirtier places of China, and I don't mind showing up in a city only to find out the plans of the Chinese have changed drastically. When my in-laws visited us in China when I was doing language study, my father in-law observed me in action and later told my wife, "Mike is the most adventurous man I know." I thank God for His work in my life, in blessing me with a job that I'd do for free because I love it so much. I always enjoy looking back at God's plan, to see how He's worked so clearly in my life.

China Resource Center Beginnings

The China Resource Center has a very clear and simple mission: We exist to deeply impact China for Christ. Our mission statement reads: Reflecting the relevance and love of Jesus Christ, we exist to equip and strengthen the growing Chinese church and to foster constructive Western engagement in China. I believe that our mission is the result of God's work in my life over the last twenty years. I often tell people that the China Resource Center is like a car that you build from a kit in your garage. Over the last twenty years, God has given me the pieces of the 'car,' one at a time, as he has built something to use for His Glory. He has used so many pieces to build the mission into what it is today. From my first introduction to Chinese students at Colorado State University in 1988, to my first trip to China in 1996, God created within me a deep heart for China and the Chinese.

In 1996, I made my first trip to China, which was a wonderful time of discovery and wonder. One story will always stand out in my mind from this first trip to China. The trip was designed as a 'vision trip,' and the organizers gave us a broad look at the cross-section of Westerners living and working in China. I remember sitting in an open air market, having a bowl of noodles with an American friend, talking about his experience in China. As we talked, a fly made a beeline into my bowl of noodles. For many Westerners, a fly makes the noodles inedible. Without missing a beat, I used the chopsticks to remove the fly, and I just continued eating the noodles as if nothing had happened. Somewhat taken aback by the nonchalant nature of my reaction to the fly, my American friend said, "You were made for this place!" I quickly gained a high standing among the American contingent in this city as the story spread, and I'm proud to say that I've been 'one of them' ever since.

As I look back at our ministry and how God has developed it into what it is today, two significant things happened in my journey. The first thing very significant event took place in 1998. My wife and I had just gotten married. We moved to Birmingham, Alabama to minister to Chinese International students at the University of Alabama-Birmingham (UAB) with a ministry called The Navigators. We were excited to invest our lives into the Chinese, and we really poured ourselves into the ministry. We both spent a significant amount of time with these Chinese intellectuals, which developed our understanding of Chinese culture. God really used that time to press me to Chinese language study. I specifically remember one situation: as we often did, we hosted a group of Chinese students in our small apartment for dinner, talking and sharing life together.

After the crowd of Chinese friends began to dissipate, two Chinese guys, who were roommates on campus, stayed later than the others. They seemed out of sorts, and they clearly wanted to talk. Since they seemed particularly down and despondent, I asked them what was going on. They were discouraged by their lack of understanding in their listening comprehension of English. After all the English language study that they had done, both in China and now in Alabama, they were despondent; they felt fortunate if they understood 50% of what their professor was saying. Surprised by this, I began asking other Chinese friends if they too had this problem. I was astounded to find out that this problem was quite common among our Chinese friends, all of whom were taking graduate-level classes at UAB. I discovered that most Chinese begin their English language study in middle-school and high school. In an overwhelmingly high percentage of the cases, the English teachers at this stage in the Chinese education systems are Chinese themselves. These teachers are effective in teaching the reading and writing components of English, but they speak English poorly. Through their middle school and high school years, these Chinese students do not have the opportunity to practice their English listening comprehension, since they do not encounter native English speakers.

As I processed this information and thought of our own ministry in Birmingham, God gave me a clear realization: If they only understand 50% of what their professor says, and here I am, trying to share the Gospel in English, how much are can they understand of what I'm saying? As a result, God planted within me a strong desire to begin the process of learning Chinese. Now I can look back on that decision as a turning point. During the two years of Chinese language study I did at UAB, I also discovered their Asian Studies program; I enrolled and eventually acquired my degree in Asian Studies.

I found that I have a natural ability in Chinese language, which also stirred within me a desire to learn more Chinese. This prompted us to move to China in 2001. While I was learning about this English language situation, I also heard more and more stories of well-meaning Americans, in Birmingham and elsewhere, sharing the Gospel with Chinese students and leading those students to 'accept Christ.' After their encounter with the American, who strongly urged his Chinese friends to come to know Christ, I began interviewing these Chinese friends to see what they took away from the time. I learned that many of these Chinese had not actually come to know Christ; they didn't really understand much of what the American friend had shared with them, but they didn't want the American to lose face and feel bad. So they 'prayed' with him, to avoid causing any trouble.

God mightily used the season of 2001-2002, when we lived in Tianjin, China. He provided contacts in two sectors of society at that time. I began to meet city-level government leaders, many of whom I found to be just like government leaders anywhere around the world. They were good men and women, looking to do a good job, hoping to not get fired and to please their boss. As I began asking questions and getting to know them, I found that they were very open in friendship and possibly partnership, especially if this would help them keep their jobs.

As I began meeting with Christian leaders from both the unregistered and registered churches, I began to understand the situation of the Church in China. My curious nature led me to ask questions and pursue answers. I loved what I saw of God's work through the Church, and I felt a very strong attachment to these dear Christians and their work in China. I made it very clear to them that I would do anything possible to help them. As they came to me with requests for help, we formed the basis of our ministry with the China Resource Center.

I learned that the Chinese church was emphasizing evangelism. Some rural pastors often joke that they doing a good job as well. I have spoken with rural pastors who are baptizing 1,000 new believers every six months. Therefore, the task of bringing Christ to people in China is no longer an area where they need our help. Instead, they need access to the resources that all these Christians need to grow in their walk; they need infrastructure to accommodate all these new Christians. As many thousands come to know Christ, this creates some real challenges. While we could serve this growth and development in a multitude of ways, we have chosen to give three things our thorough focus.

China Resource Center Projects

As I began traveling out into the rural areas of Northeast and East Central China, and as I learned about their situation, one of the first things I found were people who had made a profession of faith in Christ, but didn't have a copy of the Bible available to read and study. These believers had countless amazing stories of their journey to Christ, either through a relative who came to faith, through a sickness or more likely, through the influence of a rural, traveling evangelist. But these new believers didn't have access to Bibles. The nearest Bible was two or three miles away, and they told stories of walking two or three miles to copy down portions of Scripture, taking those hand written portions of Scripture, and studying them in their own devotional time and with family. A month later, they would be back on the trail to copy down more of the Bible. This process continued for two or three years, and the believers never had Bibles of their own.

In these rural areas, two components further the need in their situation. First, most of these rural Christians make an average of only $4.00 US each month, so the available Bibles in China are cost prohibitive. On the other hand, even if they could afford the Bibles, they are not for sale in most of their localities. This is because of the Amity Printing Company's distribution network. The distribution network delivers Bibles to over seventy distribution points throughout China, who then issue them into a circular area around the large city distribution point. There are pockets of rural and therefore inaccessible territory, where the Bibles do not arrive. These two situations add to the dire need for our Bible Distribution Events. In these rural areas, their hunger for the Word of God is so evident.

After our first Bible Distribution Event in 2005, the magnitude of this project really sank in. I was on the airplane home when I was struck with the reality of what we'd just accomplished. I thought about my own walk with Christ and

169

the incalculable value that the Bible had played in the development of my walk with the Lord; it was crucial to my understanding of who Christ was in my own life. I remembered the many times I had either searched the Scriptures for an answer to prayer, or during other times of meditation and prayer, when God had so clearly used a passage of Scripture to speak truth in my life. I still cannot imagine being a believer in Jesus Christ but not having my own copy of the Bible.

As a result of our Bible Distribution Events, our research shows that each of our Bibles also impacts five people for Christ, since it becomes the family Bible in these rural areas. Grandparents, parents and children all begin to read the new family Bible. And more specifically, we've recently learned through research in areas where we've done Bible Distribution that each Bible distributed results in three conversions to Christ. Available at $3.00 each, we normally distribute Bibles in blocks of 10,000. We send a staff member along to make sure the Bibles arrive in the hands of those who need them most. We've now had the privilege of distributing over 65,000 Bibles and counting!

Our second project in rural China to serve the growth of the church is one that is very close to my heart since the impact is so great! In 2006, as we were doing our second Bible Distribution Event of the year, after our final 'celebration' dinner that signified the end of our distribution event, our cooperating Chinese pastor approached me with a special request. In one of their most rural and remote areas, they recognized a group of Christians who had no real church building in which to hold Sunday services or any other Church events. After working together with the local village government to secure the land for a new church building, he was looking for a Western partner to help them finance the building of the church. He showed me the plans for this church, and I was amazed. For about $30,000, we could help them build a church that would hold 500 people on a Sunday morning; it would have a small Bible Training Center attached to the back to train rural pastors, and it would serve as a community center for the rural village, since it would be the nicest building in the village. He asked if I was interested, and I was energized by this effective way to serve the growth of the Church in China. We're now building rural Church buildings regularly and it's become the largest growth areas of our organization. One of the best things about building churches in these rural areas is that the rural Christians are so proud of their new building; they are sure to put the Cross at the very top of the steeple, so that as many people as possible can see the Cross and thereby find the Church.

Because of their rapid growth, the Chinese rural Church represents a tree whose roots are an inch deep and a mile wide. I fully agree with this statement; the phenomenon happening in these rural areas, is creating a huge challenge. As these rural areas experience massive Christian growth, it causes a deficiency in the ranks of leadership in rural Churches. The sheer numbers of Christians without a corresponding growth in the numbers of leaders causes an increasingly uneven situation. I've spoken with rural leaders who were asked to take a leadership/pastor role, only three months after they accepted Christ as their Lord. It is difficult for a Westerner to think about such a new Christian taking much of a leadership role. Among them, I often hear stories of these leaders falling into false teaching or heresy. To serve the Chinese Church in this area, we providing 2- to 3-man Theological Training Teams that serve and teach in rural Bible training schools. Our teams, primarily Chinese pastors of North American congregations, teach for 10-days to two weeks, and they normally teach on subjects like proper Biblical Interpretation and Apologetics.

In accomplishing our mission statement, I've taken to heart one final project. It is the process of what we call 'Clarifying Western Perceptions of Christianity in China.' Simply put, I believe that many in the West have an outdated paradigm of China, her people, and her Church. It is important to clarify these perceptions. We must understand fully what God is doing in China and the changes that the Chinese government has made to open doors in China, so then we can know best how to pray for and engage in God's work in China. If we believe, for example, that it is still necessary to smuggle Bibles into China, then our actions will reflect our paradigm. But when we find out that there is no longer a need to smuggle in Bibles, our actions will reflect differently.

We can attempt to clarify Western perceptions in several ways. Our recently redesigned website plays a key part in this effort. Between my blog, our extensive on-line videos and our Truth about China site, there's a plethora of information available. In addition, The China Resource podcast, a bi-weekly radio-show type podcast has been a very effective tool as well. This book is also our attempt to clarify perceptions. Through our continued efforts to clarify Western perceptions, God is using us as a resource for the Western Church.

It is truly a privilege to serve Christ in these ways. As you can see, I do not lack passion for the work God has put before me. More information about all of our projects is available on our website at www.ChinaResourceCenter.org. There are many avenues of partnership with our work. Whether you would like to help us build churches, distribute Bibles or send pastors, we'd love to hear from you.

Appendix A: Ethical Foundations for China Service

Recognizing the changes in China, the significant growth in the Church in China and the complexity of Chinese society and its regulatory structures, we offer these guidelines for service in China and to support the Christian community in China.

We commit to the following:

1. We will demonstrate the credibility and relevance of Jesus Christ by our words and actions.

2. We will strive to respect local government and regulations; and the culture, history, and aspirations of the Chinese people.

3. We will serve the whole body of Christ in China and promote its harmony and self-sufficiency.

4. We will promote a spirit of unity in the China-concerned Christian community.

5. We will communicate accurately only information about which we have verifiable knowledge.

Addendum Notes

1. It is well understood in government circles that most Westerners are Christians, and the implication is that how we act will reflect negatively/positively on Christianity. Most China watchers agree that there is no longer a need to hide our identity as Christians. In our attempt to be relevant, are we positioning our message about Christ in reference to what the Chinese people are asking for? Do we recognize that our credibility in China is earned?

2. Are we figuring out how the system works in China? Are we investing in relationships in China? Are we being careful not to bring your own agenda before we learn of the agenda of the local Chinese agencies? Many times, the real needs of China are not the felt needs.... Where the two do coincide, the most fruitful outcomes result. Are we learning about what is already being done locally or by other outside agencies?

3. By choosing the word 'serve,' we as foreigners want to take the position of support and encouragement as Chinese Christians take the lead in the Christian community. Are we promoting the concept of indigenous Chinese Christianity? Are we recognizing the many facets of the Church in China including house church/open church, rural church/urban church and professional church/working class church, etc. and seeking to view the Church in China in its entirety? Are

we challenging ourselves to view the Church in China as a whole? Are we communicating to the Chinese and to others from the perspective of how God wants us to be a part of the reconciliation of any tensions that exist in the body of Christ? Are we figuring out how to use our resources to support the concept of self-sufficiency in the Chinese Church in a God honoring way? Are we making sure that we are not allowing outside funds to set the agenda for Christians in China? Stories like Chinese church planters that became translators for Christian organizations, and Chinese seminarians became immigrants in the West. Are we being mindful of the intended and unintended consequences of financial investment in China? Do you have an exit strategy (how the work will continue with Chinese ownership after the money and foreign involvement are gone)? Are we perpetuating need in order to raise funds?

4. Do we have a sense of transparency, and are we getting people to come to China and see for themselves what God is doing? Are we attending Conferences, actively seeking information sharing, spending more time praying for other groups, visiting other groups? Can we use Biblical based conflict resolution principles when there is a difference in approach as opposed to taking our disagreements public? We should not question others' faith or calling into ministry even when approaches in China differ. How do we develop tolerance and mutual respect among diverse ministries to China?

5. Refer to the Evangelical Council for Financial Accountability (ECFA) Standard 7.1 on Fund-Raising—Truthfulness in Communication. The standard reads, "...narrative about events must be current, complete and accurate. References to past activities or events must be appropriately dated. There must be no material omissions or exaggerations of fact or use of misleading photographs or any other commu-

nication which would tend to create a false impression or misunderstanding."

a. Have I put my information in an appropriate context? Was there an inappropriate inducement of the source? As new information comes to light, am I diligent to make it available? Am I sure my information is verifiable through reliable sources? Am I deliberately perpetuating old stereotypes (e.g. China is a police state, no Bibles available in China)? Am I corroborating my information with data from other reliable sources? Are we aware of potential conflict of interest, either because of fund-raising needs, organizational agendas, etc.?

www.chinaresourcecenter.org